◀ SPEARHEA

7th ARMOURED DIVISION

The 'Desert Rats'

The most widely used LAA gun was the 40mm Bofors, as seen here. This one was part of the garrison at Bir Hacheim in 1942, supporting the French garrison there who kept Rommel at bay for many days, during the fighting for the Gazala line.

SPEARHEAD

7th ARMOURED DIVISION
The 'Desert Rats'

George Forty

Ian Allan
PUBLISHING

Acknowledgements

Editor: George Grant
Design: Tony Stocks
Maps: Mark Franklin
Photos: All come from the Author's collection except the colour material on pages 66, 70/71, 74/75 and 78/79, which are all courtesy of Martin Brayley.
Thanks to Jonathan Forty who did much of the preparatory work on the In Action section.

Picture Credits
All photographs in this book come from the Author's Collection except where otherwise stated.

Cover: Cruiser tanks of 7th Armoured Division meet Light Mk VIs on a desert track. All are marked with the British red/white/red identification markings.

Right: The Greater Egyptian Jerboa (*Jaculus Orientalis*), found in the desert sands of Arabia. Like all jerboas, this hardy little creature has pale, sandy-coloured fur, large eyes, tiny front legs and huge back feet that it uses to jump six feet or more in a single bound.

First published 2003

ISBN 0 7110 2988 1

© Compendium Publishing, 2003

Published by Ian Allan Ltd

an imprint of Ian Allan Publishing Ltd, Hersham, Surrey KT12 4RG
Printed by Ian Allan Printing Ltd, Hersham, Surrey KT12 4RG

Code: 0310/A2

British Library Cataloguing in Publication Data
A CIP catalogue record for this book is available from the British Library

Note: Website information provided in the Reference section was correct when provided by the author. The publisher can accept no responsibility for this information becoming incorrect.

Abbreviations

2IC	Second-in-Command
AA	Anti-aircraft
ACV	Armoured Command Vehicle
ADMS	Assistant Director Medical Services
Armd	Armoured
Arty	Artillery
Atk	Anti-tank
BD	Battledress
Bde	Brigade
BM	Brigade Major
Bn	Battalion
Bty	Battery
'Cherry Pickers'	11th Hussars
Cheshires	Cheshire Regiment
CIGS	Chiefs of the Imperial General Staff
C-in-C	Commander-in-Chief
CLY	County of London Yeomanry
CO	Commanding Officer
Coy	Company
CRASC	Commander Royal Army Service Corps
CV	Command Vehicle
DAK	Deutsches Afrika Korps
DAQMG	Deputy Assistant Quartermaster General
Derbys Yeo	Derbyshire Yeomanry
Devons	Devonshire Regiment
DG	Dragoon Guards
DLI	Durham Light Infantry
DMT	Director Military Training
DR	Dispatch Rider
EME	Electrical and Mechanical Engineers
Engrs	Engineers
Fd Amb	Field Ambulance
Fd Coy	Field Company
Fd Hygiene Sect	Field Hygiene Section
Fd Pk Sqn	Field Park Squadron
Fd Regt	Field Regiment
FDS	Field Delivery Squadron
Fd Sqn	Field Squadron
Fd Transfusion Unit	Field Transfusion Unit
FSS	Field Security Section
FSU	Field Surgical Unit
Fwd Del Sqn	Forward Delivery Squadron
GOC	General Officer Commanding
GSO	General Staff Officer
H	Hussars
Hy	Heavy
Ind Div	Indian Division
Innis	Inniskilling
Int Sect	Intelligence Section
KDG	King's Dragoon Guards
KRRC	King's Royal Rifle Corps
LAA	Light Anti-aircraft
LMG	Light Machine Gun
LO	Liaison Officer
LST	Landing Ship Tank
Lt Fd Amb	Light Field Ambulance
Lt Hygiene Sect	Light Hygiene Section
Med Regt	Medium Regiment
MELF	Middle East Land Forces
MG	Machine Gun
MMG	Medium Machine Gun
Mobile CCS	Mobile Casualty Clearing Section
Mob Dental Unit	Mobile Dental Unit
Mot	Motor
M&V	"Meat and Veg" = Beef Stew
NAAFI	Navy, Army, Air Force Institutes = canteen/general stores
Nor Yeo	Norfolk Yeomanry
OFP	Ordnance Field Park
OP	Observation Post
Ord	Ordnance
PIAT	Projector Infantry Anti-tank
Pro Coy	Provost Company
PU	Pick-up

CONTENTS

Origins & History 6

Ready for War 10

In Action 15

Insignia, Clothing & Equipment 66

People 80

Postwar 86

Assessment 89

Reference 92

Index 96

PzKpfw	Panzerkampfwagen	RHQ	Regimental Headquarters	'Skins	5th Royal Inniskilling Dragoon Guards
QMG	Quartermaster General				
RA	Royal Artillery	RIDG	Royal Inniskilling Dragoon Guards	SMLE	Short Magazine Lee Enfield (rifle)
RAC	Royal Armoured Corps				
RAMC	Royal Army Medical Corps	RMA	Royal Military Academy	SOME	Staff Officer Mechanical Engineering
		RNF	Royal Northumberland Fusiliers	SP	Self-propelled
RAOC	Royal Army Ordnance Corps				
		R Scots Greys	Royal Scots Greys	Sp Coy	Support Company
RASC	Royal Army Service Corps	RSM	Regimental Sergeant Major	Sqn	Squadron
				SSM	Squadron Sergeant-Major
RB	Rifle Brigade	RTC	Royal Tank Corps		
RE	Royal Engineers	RTR	Royal Tank Regiment	S&T	Supply & Transport
REME	Royal Electrical and Mechanical Engineers	SAAC	South African Armoured Corps	Tac	Tactical
				TCV	Troop Carrying Vehicle
RGH	Royal Gloucestershire Hussars	SD	Service Dress	Tps	Troops
		SG	Scots Guards	WDF	Western Defence Force
RHA	Royal Horse Artillery	Sigs	Signals	Wksp	Workshops

ORIGINS & HISTORY

Above: This is a woodcut of the original drawing by Mrs Peyton, wife of the division's first GSO3, from which the very first "Desert Rat" flash was produced in 1940 — see Equipment and Markings chapter for more details.

"CREATE AN ARMOURED DIVISION"

"In 1938, the year of the Munich crisis, an officer was flown from England to Egypt on an important mission: 'Create an Armoured Division' ... those were his orders." That extract from the *Egyptian Mail* for Wednesday, 10 February 1943, then goes on to outline how Maj-Gen Percy Cleghorn Stanley Hobart ("Hobo" as he was known — but never called — by everyone in the Royal Tank Corps) produced the first of the three great armoured divisions that he would be responsible for raising and training during World War II — namely, the 7th, 11th and 79th. He had to start with the "prehistoric" vehicles, weapons and equipment, which at that time made up the units of the Cairo Cavalry Brigade. As the threat of war became more and more apparent, the implications of the German-Italian Axis that had been forged in September 1936 became more and more evident, namely that the Italians might well take action to threaten the Suez Canal, that vital life-line of the British Empire. There were already large numbers of Italian troops in Cyrenaica, directly on the western border of Egypt, and Mussolini was already making bombastic noises. Therefore, to counter this potential threat, on 17 September 1938 the Cairo Cavalry Brigade was hurriedly ordered to Mersa Matruh, some 170 miles west of Alexandria, to form the "Matruh Mobile Force" under the command of Brig H. E. Russell. Its initial composition was:

HQ Cairo Cavalry Brigade & Signals

3rd Regiment Royal Horse Artillery (3 RHA), equipped with 3.7in howitzers, towed by Dragons.

7th Queen's Own Hussars (7 H), with two squadrons of light tanks, Mark III to Mark VIIB (but with no .5in ammunition for their heavy machine guns.

8th King's Royal Irish Hussars (8 H), with Ford 15cwt pick-up trucks, mounting Vickers-Berthier guns.

11th Hussars (Prince Albert's Own) (11 H), with 1920s-vintage Rolls-Royce armoured cars and a few Morrises.

1st Battalion Royal Tank Corps (1 RTC) (to be renamed 1st Royal Tank Regiment [1 RTR] after the creation of the Royal Armoured Corps [RAC] on 4 April 1939). It was newly-arrived from England, complete with 58 light tanks, but with little track mileage left and few new tracks available.

No 5 Company, Royal Army Service Corps (RASC).

2nd/3rd Field Ambulance, Royal Army Medical Corps (RAMC).

Left behind in Cairo, on internal security duties, was the 6th Battalion, Royal Tank Corps, equipped with obsolete old medium and light tanks, whilst already at Mersa Matruh was the 2nd Field Company, Royal Engineers (RE) with whom the brigade would co-operate.

Air support for this motley collection of outdated vehicles and weaponry was equally prehistoric, viz: No 108 (Army Co-operation) Squadron RAF, equipped with Hawker Audaxes; No 80 (Fighter) Squadron RAF, equipped with Gloster Gladiators and No 45 (Bomber) Squadron RAF, equipped with Hawker Harts. The arrival of a flight of Bristol Blenheims from Iraq caused great excitement!

So this was the "Mobile Force", sometimes also known rather unkindly as the "Immobile Farce", which Maj-Gen Hobart came out from England to change into an armoured division and to command. He had already shown himself to be a superlative armoured trainer on Salisbury Plain in the early 1930s, commanding the first (and only) Tank Brigade from 1931 to 1935. In 1937 he had been appointed Director of Military Training (DMT) at the War Office, an appointment about which he had grave misgivings because of the "bad attitude" towards tanks prevailing at that time in the British Army. His year as DMT had not been an easy one and he had made many enemies, especially among those who still held old fashioned views on mechanisation. These included even the Secretary of State for War (Duff Cooper), who had apologised to the Cavalry in 1936, when they had begun to mechanise, with the words: "It is like asking a great musical performer to throw away his violin and devote himself to the gramophone!" Such stupidity at so high a level would leave the British Army woefully short of tanks when war came. "Hobo", who was not one to suffer fools gladly, was naturally a passionate supporter of the tank and of armoured warfare, so he was bound to be at loggerheads with such views. He also detested the pomp and circumstance of prewar Army life. On his arrival in Cairo, the then GOC-in-C Lt-Gen Sir Robert Gordon-Finlayson had greeted him with the words: "I don't know what you've come here for, and I don't want you anyway!" Nevertheless, "Hobo" typically did not let this open hostility deter him and immediately set about transforming the Mobile Division into a formidable fighting force.

After carrying out a few exercises in the desert around Mersa Matruh, the Force returned to Cairo, where it was joined by its first infantry element, the 1st Battalion, the King's Royal Rifle Corps (1 KRRC). "Hobo" then set about the difficult task of organising from scratch the formation, training, equipment and administration of the "Mobile Division (Egypt) and Abbassia District", as the Force was now called. He wrote: "I decided to concentrate on dispersion, flexibility and mobility … to try to get the Division and formations well extended, really handy and under quick control. To units unused to speed and wide frontages made possible by mechanisation, these matters presented considerable difficulties." Throughout the summer the fledgling division held indoor exercises and hammered out in theory every aspect of the administration of an armoured force that would be so important in an inhospitable desert setting. Once the weather was cooler, the division went back to the desert again, learning how to live and fight in these difficult conditions. As always, it also had to suffer the strictures that affected peacetime soldiering — despite the fact that war was imminent — such as strictly limited track mileage for tanks, and a desperate shortage of wheeled vehicles.

"Hobo" had continually to fight against a great deal of obstruction, ignorance and

Below: Maj-Gen P. C. S. Hobart taking an early morning ride near Cairo, with his stepson Robin Chater, soon after their arrival in Egypt. "Hobo" was the best trainer of armoured units in the British Army and had just finished a tour as Director Military Training at the War Office. He was disliked and distrusted by the very conservatively minded senior officers in command in Egypt, as a result of which he was quite outrageously sacked.

Above: The original Mobile Division drawn up on parade near Mersa Matruh in 1939. Despite its outdated, obsolescent equipment, "Hobo" turned it into a highly effective, mobile force, which, as an integral part of the Western Desert Force, would do exceptionally well against the Italians.

even idleness, but his enthusiasm and determination never flagged. The difference between the Mobile Division of August 1939 and the "Immobile Farce" of just a year earlier was truly remarkable. However, he was still thwarted at every turn, especially by senior officers who simply did not understand modern war.

As well as gaining much-needed expertise in the art of mobile armoured warfare, the division also received some new equipment: 7th Hussars, for example, was now complete with three squadrons of light tanks, whilst 8th Hussars had begun to receive light tanks from 7th Hussars to replace its 15cwt pick-ups. 3rd RHA now had half 37mm anti-tank guns and half 25-pounders, and a 25-pounder battery of 4th RHA had been attached to the division to provide extra gunner support. 11th Hussars had received more Morris armoured cars and 6 RTR its first 10 A9 cruiser tanks. The order of battle now was:

Light Brigade (Commander: Brig H. E. Russell) — 7th, 8th and 11th Hussars
Heavy Brigade (Commander: Lt-Col H. R. B. Watkins) — 1st and 6th RTR
Pivot Group (Commander: Lt-Col W. H. B. Mirrles) — 3rd RHA, F Battery
    4th RHA and 1st KRRC

Once war had broken out with Germany, the division went on another series of exercises under the watchful eye of "Hobo", returning to Cairo once again in November 1939. Gordon-Finlayson's place had now been taken by Gen "Jumbo" Wilson, with whom "Hobo" initially got on very amicably until one particular exercise, when a series of misunderstandings arose between them. These were mainly due to the fact that, like most successful armoured commanders, "Hobo" led from the front and was therefore never available at his HQ, where more orthodox commanders like Wilson expected to find him. This led to a personal row which resulted in Wilson writing to Gen Wavell (then C-in-C Middle East) saying that he no longer had any confidence in Hobart and asking for him to be relieved of his command. So "Hobo" left without further ado. It is interesting to note that Gen O'Connor who, as commander of the Western Desert Force, had worked closely with Gen Hobart on the desert exercises, had had no difficulties working with him and expressed the opinion that the Mobile Division was the best trained division he had ever seen. In his book about his wartime career (*Eight Years Overseas 1939-1947*) Wilson makes no mention of their disagreement, merely just stating that Hobart was relieved by Creagh during the winter. A measure of the high esteem in which he was held by the men of his division can be judged by the fact that without any orders being issued, the men of the Mobile Division lined the route as he left his headquarters to bid him farewell. "Hobo" went back to the temporary obscurity of retirement, exchanging his general's badges of rank for those of a lance corporal in his local Home Guard — fortunately, however, not for long, Winston Churchill personally going "into bat" for him. "I think highly of this officer," Churchill wrote to the CIGS on 19 October 1940, "and am not at all impressed by the prejudices against him in certain quarters. Such prejudices attach frequently to persons of strong personality and original view. In this case General Hobart's original views have been only too tragically borne out. The neglect by the General Staff even to devise proper patterns of tanks before the war has robbed us of all the fruits of this invention. These fruits have been reaped by the enemy with terrible consequences. We should therefore remember that this was an officer who had the root of the matter in him, and also the vision."

Maj-Gen Hobart's place was taken by Maj-Gen Michael O'Moore Creagh (late 15/19 H), but his influence remained long after his departure and many times his views were quoted — "'Hobo' used to say …". As Maj-Gen Verney said of him, in the prologue to his history of the division: "His departure came as a rude shock to the Division. To his country the General's services had been considerable, to the Division he formed and trained they were immeasurable and the long record of success in the years that followed stands as a tribute to their first commander."

Above: Light MkVI tanks of 1 RTR on manoeuvres near the Pyramids, 24 January 1939. Despite being of little use in battle, these tiny, light tanks were ideal as training vehicles for the Mobile Division, and, despite being restricted on track mileage, they enabled the division to acquire a great deal of desert experience.

REDESIGNATION

More changes followed the departure of "Hobo". The Heavy Brigade became 4th Armoured Brigade and the Light Brigade, the 7th Armoured Brigade; the Pivot Group became officially known as the Support Group and was enlarged with the arrival from Palestine of the 2nd Battalion the Rifle Brigade (2 RB). 3 RHA was converted into an anti-tank regiment and 4 RHA complete joined the division, together with 2 RTR and other units from the UK. Brig J. A. L. Caunter, late RTR, took command of 4th Armd Bde. On 16 February 1940, the Mobile Division was officially redesignated as the 7th Armoured Division. War against Italy now became a distinct possibility, so the division moved light forces up to the frontier wire.

AND ON TOWARDS WAR

When, towards the end of April 1940, it became obvious that Italy was going to enter the war the 11th Hussars and the Support Group moved out to Mersa Matruh. In the middle of May they were followed by divisional headquarters and 4th Armd Bde. For another month intensive training continued, together with surreptitious reconnaissance of the Italian frontier posts (undertaken only by the squadron commanders of 11th Hussars). These had to be very carefully done as they were under orders to do nothing that might be considered provocative. 11th Hussars also had to get used to maintaining its subunits on a very wide front — the distance between regimental headquarters and squadrons being some 60 to 80 miles. This necessitated reorganising its unit transport on a double echelon basis. Everyone was stretched to the limits, so the welcome arrival of some volunteers from Southern Rhodesia was much appreciated. Forty-five of these volunteers went to 11 H and were formed into Scout Troops in Ford cars.

READY FOR WAR

ITALY DECLARES WAR

At 7pm on the evening of 10 June 1940, Il Duce declared war on Great Britain and France. He had been agonising what to do for some days, trying to decide whether or not to throw his lot in with the Axis or to remain neutral. "If we have decided to face the risks and sacrifices of war, it is because the honour and interest of Italy requires it of us." What that really meant was that he could not wait any longer to share in the "spoils of war" which would begin to satisfy his thirst for glory. Once the British had been forced to retreat from Dunkirk and the German Blitzkrieg had swept through most of France, Mussolini made his decision and opted for the Axis camp. Clearly he had designs on "empire building" in North Africa, despite naming Egypt among the neighbours whom Italy did not intend to: "… drag into conflict". Indeed, when the Italian envoy HE Nobile Serafine dei Conti Mazzolini, Envoy Extraordinary and Minister Plenipotentiary of Italy in Egypt, had been given his marching orders when Egypt broke off diplomatic relations, Mazzolini had said, with a knowing look: "We shall be back in a fortnight," and had left his car and his entire wardrobe behind!

Below: Radio vehicles and their crews belonging to RHQ 1 RTR pause during an exercise in the desert during the late spring of 1939. The use of radio was very much in its infancy before war began and wirelesses were still not widely issued within the British Army, except within armoured units and other mobile troops. Even within a tank squadron, troop commanders invariably used hand signals to control their troops so as to reduce radio transmissions, but were in touch with their squadron commander via the radio.

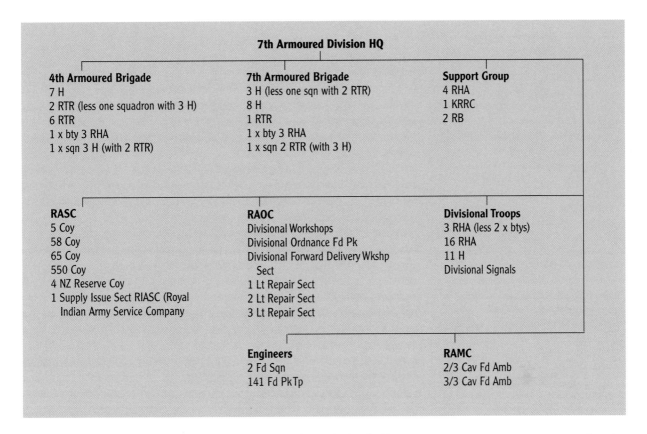

7th Armoured Division HQ

4th Armoured Brigade	**7th Armoured Brigade**	**Support Group**
7 H	3 H (less one sqn with 2 RTR)	4 RHA
2 RTR (less one squadron with 3 H)	8 H	1 KRRC
6 RTR	1 RTR	2 RB
1 x bty 3 RHA	1 x bty 3 RHA	
1 x sqn 3 H (with 2 RTR)	1 x sqn 2 RTR (with 3 H)	

RASC	**RAOC**	**Divisional Troops**
5 Coy	Divisional Workshops	3 RHA (less 2 x btys)
58 Coy	Divisional Ordnance Fd Pk	16 RHA
65 Coy	Divisional Forward Delivery Wkshp	11 H
550 Coy	Sect	Divisional Signals
4 NZ Reserve Coy	1 Lt Repair Sect	
1 Supply Issue Sect RIASC (Royal	2 Lt Repair Sect	
Indian Army Service Company	3 Lt Repair Sect	

	Engineers	**RAMC**
	2 Fd Sqn	2/3 Cav Fd Amb
	141 Fd PkTp	3/3 Cav Fd Amb

The following day the complete 7th Armoured Division moved up to the frontier. Between its first move up to the frontier on 11 June and the first major operation conducted by the Western Desert Force, of which the Division formed a major part, in early December, it received some reinforcements. For example, 2 RTR left the UK on 20 August and arrived in mid-October. Equipped with A13s, plus some A9s and A10s, the Second entrained immediately for the Western Desert, where it joined 4th Armd Bde. Thus the divisional order of battle at the start of Operation Compass is shown in the table above.

Above: Divisional organisation as at November 1940.

MAIN COMPONENTS

Divisional Headquarters In the early days, Div HQ was divided into two main groups or echelons — Advanced and Rear. Advanced HQ (later known as Main HQ) contained only those necessary for the control and command of the division during operations; in other words, the GOC, his "G" and "I" staffs, artillery and engineer advisers, together with the crews of the communications and protection vehicles. Before the Command vehicles were armoured, two armoured cars were also included in this group, so that a Battle HQ (later called Tactical HQ) could be formed and all unarmoured vehicles withdrawn when action was imminent.

Rear Division contained the rest of Div HQ, that is to say everything that was not required for immediate operational control. The Heads of the Services (CRASC, ADMS, SOME, etc) worked here under the AA & QMG. Their duties were mainly concerned with the control and direction of the administration of the division. Rear HQ was usually located some distance behind Advanced HQ, where it could work free from the risk of enemy ground interference.

ADVANCED HQ ON MOVE

3 x Cruiser Tanks — Protective
Detachment
1 x Armoured Car — Navigator

Group "A"
ACV 1 — Command ACV
(nerve centre of Div HQ)
Despatch rider on a motorcycle
ACV 2 — Intelligence ACV
ACV 3 — Rear Link
1 x Scout Car

Group "B" (160yd behind)
1 x Cruiser tank — GOC's Charger
Despatch rider on a motorcycle
1 x Cruiser tank — "G" Charger
1 x Armoured Car — "Q" Charger
1 x Scout Car

Group "C" (160yd behind)
ACV 4 — Spare ACV
1 x Scout Car
3 x Ford PU — Liaison Officers

Group "D" (160yd behind)
Office Truck — G Office
Office Truck — Signals Office
Despatch rider on a motorcycle
Ford PU — Frontier Force

When on the move, Advanced HQ moved in groups, as shown in the box at left.(When stationary it formed a scattered leaguer, closing into a tight box formation.)

Reconnaissance The Divisional Armoured Car Regiment (11 H) had the task of providing distant recce, anything up to 50 miles from the main body of the division. This difficult and dangerous work had to be undertaken in any direction — to the front, flanks, even, on some occasions, to the rear. There could never be any gaps of time or space in the recce screen, as a constant up-to-the-minute flow of information was essential. The regiment therefore had to be able to split into a large number of small independent patrols, each capable of operating on its own for extended periods. It was also necessary for a centrally held reserve to be maintained at squadron level to meet unexpected situations and allow time, in theory anyway, for vehicle maintenance.

To tackle this considerable task, the regiment consisted of three reconnaissance squadrons, each of five troops of three armoured cars, although on some occasions a fourth recce sqn was added. Armoured car troops acted as the eyes and ears of the recce screen, with the rest of the regiment in control and supporting roles. Radio communications were its lifeblood, so that the unceasing flow of vital information could be passed swiftly back to higher formation. Despite numerous changes of vehicles and terrain, the basic task remained unchanged throughout the war and the 11th Hussars remained the "eyes of the division" throughout hostilities.

Armour The most powerful tactical unit of the division was the armoured regiment. The organisation of these armoured regiments together with the numbers and types of tanks they contained varied considerably during the war years. For details of these see pages 72–3. Initially there were three types of tanks in vogue: small light tanks, generally only armed with machine guns, whose main task was reconnaissance; medium-sized, fast, lightly armoured cruiser tanks, whose main role was to exploit breakthroughs and spread havoc behind enemy lines; finally, heavily armoured, slow moving infantry tanks to support major assaults, in what was still basically an infantry-orientated army. As the war progressed, the role of light tanks was taken over almost entirely by armoured cars/light recce vehicles, whilst the heavy infantry tanks were taken out of armoured divisions and organised into independent tank brigades. This left the cruiser tank as the main equipment of the armoured division — an unhappy situation due to its poor firepower

Left: Light tanks of 1 RTR are seen here on yet another parade, possibly the Royal Review of 1939 for King Farouk of Egypt. He had ascended to the throne in 1936 and ruled Egypt until 1952 when his regime was overthrown by Gamal Abdel Nasser. During the war, Farouk tried unsuccessfully to maintain neutrality despite the presence of British troops.

Below left: Echelon vehicle crews of 1 RTR line up for a briefing. Note all wear their respirators in the ready position; also all wear steel helmets. The NCO doing the talking has his pistol slung low on a special webbing strap and tied around the thigh like a Wild West gunfighter. Until the Sten gun and Thompson submachine gun became more widely available, the .38 pistol was the most commonly issued weapon for tank crews.

and woefully thin armour. Fortunately, however, help was at hand, the USA generously supplying firstly better-armed, more reliable, light tanks (the M3 Light, known officially as the Stuart in British service, but nicknamed the "Honey" by the crews), then Mediums (M3 Lee/Grant and M4 Sherman) with their 75mm guns and thicker armour, their main gun having both anti-tank and anti-personnel capability — the first time that British tanks had been armed with such a large-calibre weapon in quantity since 1918! Eventually, the cruiser and the Medium tank lines became indistinguishable in firepower, protection and mobility, Comet and Centurion being the end of the cruiser line and the beginning of the medium gun/main battle tank line that has progressed through Chieftain and Challenger 1, to the modern-day Challenger 2, which has performed so well in the latest war in Iraq.

Below: Moving up to Mersa Matruh. This tank train, loaded with light tanks of 1 RTR, was photographed at Fuka, en route to Mersa Matruh. Using the railway saved on track mileage, which was very strictly limited (for monetary reasons) even when troops were preparing for war.

Above: Cruiser tanks of 2 RTR on their way "Up the Blue". 2 RTR arrived in Egypt from the UK in mid-October and entrained immediately for its move to Mersa Matruh, where it joined the 4th Armd Bde of 7th Armoured Division.

A FORMATION OF ALL ARMS

From the outset it must be appreciated that an armoured division is a formation of all arms. "Tanks by themselves cannot win battles, so the unarmoured units of the armoured division are just as indispensable as the armoured ones, whilst the administrative services play roles no less vital and equally dangerous in maintaining supplies of all kinds, and in dealing with casualties to men and vehicles. Each arm or branch of service is a member of a team and has its vital part to play. Mutual understanding and confidence, based on experience during training and during action, form the keystone to success." These down-to-earth words of wisdom appeared in a wartime Military Training Pamphlet and must have been well appreciated, understood and followed by every member of the 7th Armoured Division throughout its wartime existence. The tank would finish World War II in a pre-eminent place on the land battlefield and has lost none of its usefulness during the turbulent days of peace that have followed. However, what must never be forgotten is that it is teamwork by a force of all arms that wins battles — and this was the case from the very first minor engagement that took place "Up the Blue" in the trackless wastes of the Western Desert.

Infantry The infantry will always be a vital component of any properly balanced fighting force and this was certainly the case in 7th Armoured Division. Tanks can capture ground, then dominate it for limited periods, but need infantry support if they are to hold for long or sustain their attacks. Within the division there were two types of infantry — a motor battalion and a mounted infantry brigade. The former was an integral part of the armoured brigade and its soldiers were experts at working closely with tanks (cf German Panzergrenadiers) and invariably travelled into battle in half-tracks, but dismounted to fight. They also had a high proportion of armoured scout carriers, scout cars and SP or towed anti-tank guns, so they could and did, provide immediate infantry support. On the other hand, the mounted infantry brigade at best travelled in lorries (TCVs), which made their speed on roads and good tracks even faster than that of the AFVs they were supporting. However, they were not tactically mounted so had to be careful not to expose their lorries to direct enemy fire .

Artillery Within the armoured division all three types of artillery — field, anti-tank and light anti-aircraft — had to be able to move at the same speed as the armour. Therefore, unlike German artillery which was horse-drawn in many instances, British artillery was motorised (towed by a tractor in which the gun crew travelled) or self-propelled. Lighter guns were initially carried "portee" — that is to say, in the back of an open truck (eg 2pdr anti-tank). Medium and heavy artillery might well be used to support the division but was never an integral part of its basic organisation.

Engineers Whatever the phase of war — advance, attack, defence or withdrawal — the Engineers were constantly needed. Their primary role was to assist the division in maintaining its mobility, so they had to be able to deal with a wide variety of natural obstacles (by preparing diversions, building bridges, etc) as well as dealing with enemy demolitions, booby traps and minefields — in fact, anything that hampered the division's progress. Additionally they were responsible for many other engineering tasks, which in the desert included the vital supply of water. In defence, they carried out specialist engineer tasks, like laying and recording minefields, or building defences and strongpoints.

Signals Communications were the lifeblood of any mobile armoured force and it is no exaggeration to say that the successful operation of an armoured division — especially in the desert — depended upon reliable communications. The system had to be flexible enough to meet any situation that arose, especially since fighting a mobile battle over vast areas of trackless desert wastes produced new problems hourly. The Royal Signals were responsible for communications at divisonal and brigade headquarters and down to units. Within units it was the responsibility of regimental signallers. All types of communications were used — wireless, land line and message carriers (LOs, DRs etc). Wireless provided the fastest and most flexible means but was dependent upon the skill of operators, the range of the radio sets and on the amount of outside interference, both climatic and from enemy jamming. Codes and ciphers had to be used as the enemy could, and did, listen in.

The Services The armoured division was a formation of all arms, in which the administrative services played no less a vital and dangerous role as the "teeth" arms. So "A" and "Q" Services, which included supplies and transport, medical and dental, ordnance, EME repair and recovery, provost and field security, pay, postal, welfare (eg NAAFI), chaplains and all the rest, played their part in keeping the division fighting fit and able to fight efficiently no matter the circumstances.

IN ACTION

"A PLACE FIT ONLY FOR WAR"

That is how the Western Desert of North Africa has been somewhat cynically described, so it is well worth looking briefly at the geography of the area in which the campaigns of the ensuing two and half years took place. It consisted of a level inland desert plateau stepping down in steep escarpments to a narrow coastal plain approximately 30 miles in width. The endpoints of these escarpments (south of Sidi Barrani and west of Tobruk), and their main gaps (Alamein, Halfaya near Sollum and Sidi Rezegh just south of Tobruk), along with the (only metalled) vital coast road connecting the two opposing capitals (Cairo and Tripoli), were to become the main focus of the actions that took place.

The climate of the area spanned the extremes of heat and cold within each 24-hour period, while the inimical desert terrain harboured winds and dust storms, thinly crusted impassable sand seas and other hazards. Yet for all its harshness, few were left untouched by the desert's austere beauty.

For both sides the problems of maintenance, recovery and supply were paramount, with all *matériel* having to be transported into the battle area. Water, fuel, ammunition and spares were always critical, while rations were often minimal and rarely followed army norms. "Living off the land" was impossible, but to capture a portion of the other side's supplies could prove to be a fortunate, at times even a life-saving, bonus. The logistics of these operations were to accelerate the development of new arms of service organisations, that would include the formation of the Corps of Royal Electrical and Mechanical Engineers (formed under Army Order 70 of 1942) to provide specialist electrical and mechanical servicing and repairs for the increasingly mechanised Army.

Below: Light tanks exercising with infantry. The white "24" shows that these light Mark VIs belong to 1 RTR. They are exercising with men of the 1/6 Rajputana Rifles of 4th Indian Division, as they prepare for Operation Compass, Gen O'Connor's daring raid on the Italian forts. Unbeknown to all but the "top brass", O'Connor had caused dummy forts to be built in a similar layout to those constructed by the Italians, so that everyone knew precisely what to do when battle was joined. *IWM — E777*

THE FIRST OFFENSIVE — OPERATION COMPASS

C-in-C MELF, Gen Archibald Wavell, made the most of the strategic asset of the railway connecting Alexandria to Mersa Matruh and adopted a policy of defence in depth, with infantry based on the defended railhead and aggressive patrolling by 7th Armoured Division lying immediately

Above: "Piccadilly Circus." This well-known track junction, in the desert south of Sidi Barrani not only had its own signpost but also, as the photograph shows, its own statue of Eros! "Charing Cross" was the name given by the troops to another important cross tracks, whilst "Marble Arch" was the troops' name for the Italian triumphal arch (*Arco del Felini*) on the coast road.

behind the frontier wire. He was seeking to contain the massive Italian army on Egypt's western frontier (consisting of five divisions in Cyrenaica backed up by nine more in Tripolitania — a total of over 215,000 men), with a force less than a third its size.

In fact the excellent training and ethos of Gen Hobart, coupled with the attacking instincts of Gen O'Connor and his staff, enabled these hurriedly cobbled together elements now called the: "Western Desert Force (WDF)", to coalesce into a capable mixed force of all arms which went on to first dominate its larger enemy, then decimate and ultimately to destroy it.

The primarily unmechanised Italians chose to remain on their side of the frontier wire, in forts too far apart to cover each other properly, and to rely on their supposedly overwhelming air superiority. The moment war was declared on 11 June, the Support Group of the division and the 11th Hussars (its armoured car regiment) whipped through the border wire, into Libya and action, dominating the gaps between the Capuzzo and Maddalena forts, probing, raiding and taking ever increasing numbers of prisoners. On 14 June both forts were captured and partly destroyed. On 16 June the first tank-versus-tank encounter took place, with the Italian force being annihilated. These actions set the tempo of the whole campaign, kept the initiative with the British who through sheer aggression made the enemy think they were facing a much larger force.

For the next four months the Italians did little more than reoccupy their forts, but on 13 September Marshal Graziani finally ordered his army over the border — moving ponderously and stopping only halfway to the critical strategic objective of Mersa Matruh. Just south of Sidi Barrani on the escarpment they built some half dozen fortified camps, content to have symbolically occupied British territory.

For the next three months, with the Italians static, the WDF continued harassing and maintaining the initiative, using its mobile forces, such as 7th Armoured Division's armoured cars and "Jock Columns". The latter were named after the then Lt-Col "Jock" Campbell of 4 RHA who would go on to command 7th Armoured Division, be awarded the Victoria Cross and be killed in a car accident in the desert in February 1942. These columns consisted of a few field guns, some anti-tank guns carried "portee" in the backs of lorries, some armoured cars and up to a company of motorised infantry. They were used in a highly mobile role to penetrate behind enemy lines, disrupt and destroy his communications and supply lines, and to build up through excellent reconnaissance an in-depth knowledge of the enemy's defences and resources.

Operation Compass This pause also gave valuable time to the WDF, to improve its supply and service echelons and to plan and practice for Operation Compass, as Gen O'Connor's proposed five-day raid on the Italian positions was now called. Practice operations were carried out against exact replicas of the Italian forts which O'Connor had caused to be built in the desert in the utmost secrecy, so that the Italians would hear nothing, but the troops taking part would know exactly what to do when the time came. Gen O'Connor launched his surprise attack on the Italian camps on the night of 7/8

Left: This light tank crew is well wrapped up against the bitter cold of an early desert morning, as it brews up a reviving cuppa. Making a brew was very easy for tank crews as they always had the means of making a small fire and could carry billy cans, etc on their AFVs. *IWM — E1501*

Below: An A13 Mark II cruiser tank belonging to 2 RTR receives some maintenance from its crew after the successful capture of Sid Omar from the Italians. The A13 Mark II was essentially just an uparmoured version of the A13, bringing its armour thickness up to 20-30mm.

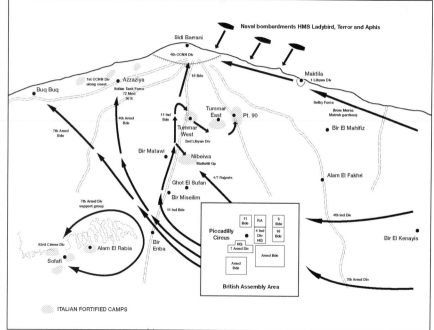

Naval bombardments HMS Ladybird, Terror and Aphis

ITALIAN FORTIFIED CAMPS

Above: Operation Compass — the capture of Sidi Barrani, 9–11 December 1940.

December 1940, moving to an Assembly Area (near "Piccadilly Circus" south of Sidi Barrani), then taking Nibeiwa and Tummar Forts with 4th Ind Div (Beresford-Pierse) supported by the Matilda MkIIs of 7 RTR, at dawn on 9 December 1940.

7th Armd Div's major roles in the operation were to cut the coast road to the west of Sidi Barrani, block the Italian escape routes from the forts and the town, and also prevent interference from other Italian forces to the west. It accomplished most of the missions without too many problems, however, one Italian formation made a stand to the west of Bug Bug, inflicting some damage with its dug-in artillery guns, before being broken and fleeing, leaving behind some four thousand prisoners. Now began an Italian retreat towards the border and back into Cyrenaica, pursued, despite the vagaries of supply, by the division followed by the rest of the WDF. To overcome salting of water sources by the enemy, fresh water and fuel was shipped in up the coast by sea.

A CHANGE OF DIVISIONS

The success of the WDF "five-day raid" led to its continuance, as first one then another of the coastal towns fell to O'Connor's forces. Progress was, however, not made any easier by the enforced removal of 4th Indian Division to East Africa. Fortunately, it was almost immediately replaced by 6th Australian Division, so the WDF — now called XIII Corps — was able to continue to maintain the pressure on the Italian garrisons as the enemy withdrew along the coast. Bardia was the next objective, with the 7th Armd Div being again used to cut the coast road and isolate the garrison from the west. It fell on 5 January 1941, yielding 45,000 prisoners. The division was then used in the same encircling movement westwards to isolate Tobruk, with the Support Group cutting the road west and the armoured brigades attacking in an arc ranged from the west to the south. Tobruk surrendered on 22 January, with another 30,000 prisoners and all their equipment taken.

It is easy to write that the division was used to encircle each of these towns, however, it is worthwhile remembering exactly what this meant to the tank crews involved, having to find their way across mainly uncharted desert wastes, over difficult, dangerous terrain, often by night and without proper maps. The wear and tear on engines, gearboxes, suspensions and all the rest of the mechanical "bits" was matched only by the pressure on the tank crews themselves to complete their vital task — otherwise the enemy would escape to live and fight another day! By now such wear and tear had reduced the division's tank strength considerably, so 8 H of 7th Armd Bde and 6 RTR of 4th Armd Bde were both temporarily dismounted and their tanks used to keep the other regiments of both brigades up to strength. The three Light Recovery Sections and a Field Supply Depot were brought forward in an attempt maximise declining resources for the next phase of the advance. As the WDF's supply line lengthened so too did the problems of maintaining its meagre resources.

Top: Ready for the great race to Beda Fomm. John March of 2 RTR, poses beside his well-laden A10 cruiser tank, before the long desert approach march to Beda Fomm. This daring manoeuvre by tanks of 7th Armoured Division cut off the Italian retreat and led to the surrender of the entire Italian Tenth Army.

Above: The advance to Benghazi and beyond, 12 December–8 February 1941. Inset, the Battle of Beda Fomm/Sidi Saleh 5–7 February 1941.

THE DESTRUCTION OF AN ARMY

By 22 January 1941, the British forces were within 20 miles of Derna, and it became clear that the Italians were preparing to leave Cyrenaica as quickly as possible, so O'Connor decided, with Wavell's blessing, upon a daring plan. He would order 7th Armoured to send a flying column through the desert to establish an armoured roadblock behind the retreating enemy, well southwest of Benghazi, in the Beda Fomm-Sidi Saleh area, whilst the rest of his force maintained pressure along the coastal route. "Combeforce" under the CO of the 11th Hussars was despatched and, despite the terrible going and several enemy air attacks en route, managed to reach the coast and cut off the Italian retreat on the morning of 5 February, at Sidi Saleh. The initial Combeforce was less than 2,000 men, mainly infantry with a few light guns and some armoured cars, but they were fortunately reinforced that afternoon by the leading elements of 4th Armd Bde (just 20 cruisers and 30 light tanks still motoring!), who established a second blocking position at nearby Beda Fomm, before the main body of the enemy arrived. The Italians were staggered to find their way blocked and, instead of trying to outflank the tiny British force, launched a series of uncoordinated frontal attacks, all of which were beaten off with heavy loss. The battle lasted until the early hours of 9 February, when the Italians surrendered. The tiny British force had by then captured 20,000 men, including six Italian generals, 216 guns, 112 tanks and 1,500 lorries, plus immense quantities of arms, equipment and stores of all kinds. The Tenth Italian Army was no more, whilst the cost to 7th Armd Div was just nine killed and 15 wounded! In less than 30 hours the "Desert Rats" had advanced across 150 miles on unmapped desert at high speed. Then, outnumbered, short of water, food, ammunition, petrol and without any prospect of reinforcement it had outfought and destroyed an army many times its strength — small wonder a leading historian called it: "one of the most daring ventures and breathless races in the annals of the British Army".

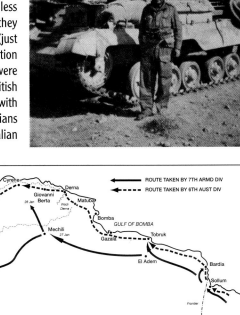

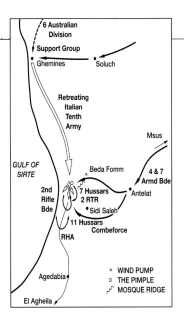

Thus ended the division's first campaign. Shortly after the victory at Beda Fomm/Sidi Saleh, it was withdrawn to refit and re-equip as its vehicles and equipment were now completely worn out.

THE DESERT 1941-2

With the surrender of the Tenth Italian Army, the whole of Cyrenaica was now in British hands and the road to Tripoli lay wide open. However, just two months later, the enemy was once again back on the Egyptian border, whilst the brilliant Gen O'Connor, plus two other senior commanders, were all "in the bag". What had caused this sudden reversal of fortunes? Undoubtedly a major shift in the strategic situation had been partly to blame, Wavell having to send considerable forces to help in the Balkans and Greece, where the Germans had once again stepped in to assist their inept Italian partners. Critical emphasis, attention and resources were switched there to counter the Axis assault. Nevertheless, Germany had not forgotten North Africa and still had ambitions to capture

Above: A pair of 25-pounders in action. This gun's primary task was the destruction or neutralisation of enemy weapons, in particular anti-tank guns and field artillery. It was widely used by field artillery and had a maximum range of 13,400yd.

Below right: Spoils of war 1. An 11th Hussars armoured car towing a captured Italian CorroVeloce 3/33. The light tankette weighed only 3.2 tons and was used to support infantry with its twin machine guns. *IWM — E408*

Egypt and cut Britain's vital Suez Canal lifeline to its empire. Early in 1941, therefore, the German High Command decided to create the *Deutsches Afrika Korps* (DAK), initially consisting of 5th leichte and 15th Panzer Divisions, and to send this force to help the Italians in Cyrenaica. To command them Hitler chose the charismatic *Generalleutnant* Erwin Rommel, who had recently sprung to fame as the GOC of the 7th (Ghost) Panzer Division in France. By the end of March 1941, Rommel, together with the leading elements of the DAK had arrived inTripoli, where he immediately assumed overall control of the Axis forces, including two Italian divisions, the Ariete and the Brescia. True to his nature, Rommel lost no time in seizing the initiative and taking the fight to the British, his initial probing reconnaissance with 5 leichte swiftly turning into a daring assault.The "Desert Fox", as he was soon called by both sides, realised that he had caught his enemy "on the hop" and immediately turned the situation to his advantage. He began to attack on 1 April, with just skeleton forces, however, by the 3rd he had taken Benghazi and on 10 April began the first siege ofTobruk (which would last for 242 days). His advance was only finally halted after it had penetrated across the Egyptian frontier near Sollum.

7th Armoured Division did not play a major part in stemming this first German assault. Having left the desert in early 1941 for some well-earned rest, the division had found itself to all intents and purposes non-existent, due to a chronic shortage of tanks and other equipment. However, faced with this new threat that was "Blitzkrieging" its way through the untested troops then holding Cyrenaica (principally 2nd Armoured and 9th Australian Divisions, augmented by 3rd Hussars and 6th RTR, who had been left behind by 7th Armoured with the few serviceable light tanks and some captured Italian mediums), other elements of the division began hastily re-equipping and were then rushed to the front. Late March saw the 1st Battalion KRRC moved up to engage the enemy near Derna and then in early April the 11th Hussars, issued with South African Marmon-Herrington armoured cars, were back in action. On 13 April the Support Group HQ was moved to Mersa Matruh, with the 3rd Battalion Coldstream Guards temporarily attached, and engaged the enemy near Sollum. The following day Brig "Strafer" Gott arrived and took over command of all troops in the area.

Rommel had thus got off to a flying start and the Axis soon had the port of Benghazi in full working order. However there was now an inevitable pause whilst the tanks of 15th Panzer were landed and the Axis forces at the front were resupplied. Gen Wavell, with encouragement from Churchill, who had responded to the German attack by diverting a convoy of fresh armour through the risky Mediterranean rather than sending it on the longer route around the safer Cape, attempted to marshal his forces for an early counteroffensive, but it took time to prepare new equipment and to train the soldiers in desert warfare.

Above: "Fox killed in the open!" That was the message sent by O'Connor to C-in-C Middle East, Gen Wavell, after the victory at Beda Fomm. Here a KDG armoured car moves past groups of knocked-out Italian vehicles and artillery guns which stretched along the coast road to Tripoli as far as the eye could see.

In the forthcoming battles there was also the emerging question of comparative merits as regards to the equipment used by each side, as well as their organisation and tactics. German armour undoubtedly had the edge over the Allies, their tank guns having better penetrative power over longer ranges, whilst their thicker armour gave them increased protection. The Panzer division was also organised on a more balanced all-arms basis, with greater flexibility of manoeuvre. There was also an imbalance in anti-tank guns, the superlative German 88mm, encountered for the first time by the British in this campaign for example, showed itself to be a battle winner, with a performance that at the time the British could not match.

Right: Divisional organisation as at April 1942.

OPERATIONS BREVITY AND BATTLEAXE

Although preliminary attacks for the possession of Halfaya Pass and Fort Capuzzo (Operation Brevity, 15-17 May) had been repulsed by a strong German counterthrust, nevertheless Operation Battleaxe finally got underway on 15 June, with 7th Armoured Division consisting of two brigades, each of two regiments, and the Support Group. In 7th Armd Bde, 2 RTR still had the old cruisers (A9s, A10S and A13s), while 6 RTR was issued with the first new A15 Crusaders , as yet untried in battle. In the 4th Armd Bde, both 4 and 7 RTR were equipped with the heavy, slow Matilda MkII "I" tanks. The plan for the division was to move in tandem with the 4th Ind Div until such a time as the 4th Armd Bde was no longer needed and then for it to swing south/southwest to cut off the enemy forces near the frontier.

In the event this never happened, for the Germans had positioned 88mm guns and laid minefields in the Sollum area, placing the recently arrived 15th Panzer Division near Bardia, with 5 leichte near Tobruk. 4th Armd Bde lost heavily to the dug-in 88s and were held down by counter-attacks; the weakened 7th Armd Bde also could not break through the skilful German defence, and, lacking a third regiment, had great difficulty even in repulsing flank counterattacks from 5 leichte. After two days' fighting, Lt-Gen Beresford-Pierse, the corps commander, called off the operation, having decided he had lost too much for too little gain.

This aborted offensive was part of a learning curve. It showed the dangers of splitting up armour across too wide a front and highlighted various other operational mistakes. It also proved that the A15 Crusader MkI, with its tiny 2pdr gun, was rather a disappointment, as compared to its opposition, in particular the German "Specials". However, combat attrition had also affected the enemy and both sides were exhausted. Neither would do much for the next four months other than continue the siege of Tobruk, while both prepared for a fresh effort.

OPERATION CRUSADER

The Commander-in-Chief, Gen Wavell, was replaced by Gen Auchinleck in early July, while Maj-Gen "Strafer" Gott, an old desert hand, assumed command of 7th Armd Div, which was increased to three armoured brigades by the addition of the 22nd. Although on paper (see table) it now appeared larger than the enemy formations opposing it, in reality the variety and quality of the armour available belied this numerical advantage. Other organisational and tactical changes in the balance of elements within each brigade were also being tried, but the correct equation for an ideally balanced armoured division had yet to be attained.

By early November 1941, sufficient reinforcements had arrived in theatre for the Army of the Nile to become the new Eighth Army, commanded by Lt-Gen Sir Alan

Below: Operation Battleaxe 15–19 June 1941.

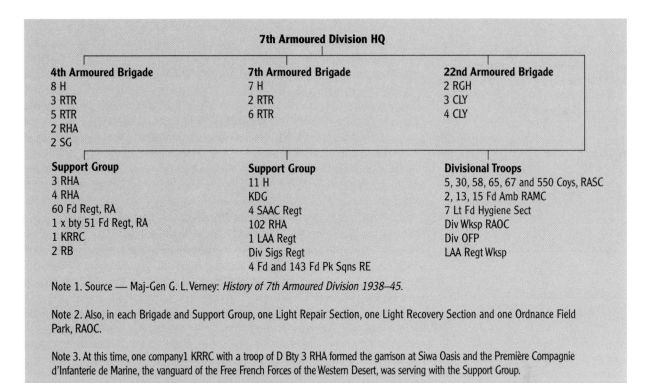

7th Armoured Division HQ		
4th Armoured Brigade	**7th Armoured Brigade**	**22nd Armoured Brigade**
8 H	7 H	2 RGH
3 RTR	2 RTR	3 CLY
5 RTR	6 RTR	4 CLY
2 RHA		
2 SG		
Support Group	**Support Group**	**Divisional Troops**
3 RHA	11 H	5, 30, 58, 65, 67 and 550 Coys, RASC
4 RHA	KDG	2, 13, 15 Fd Amb RAMC
60 Fd Regt, RA	4 SAAC Regt	7 Lt Fd Hygiene Sect
1 x bty 51 Fd Regt, RA	102 RHA	Div Wksp RAOC
1 KRRC	1 LAA Regt	Div OFP
2 RB	Div Sigs Regt	LAA Regt Wksp
	4 Fd and 143 Fd Pk Sqns RE	

Note 1. Source — Maj-Gen G. L. Verney: *History of 7th Armoured Division 1938–45.*

Note 2. Also, in each Brigade and Support Group, one Light Repair Section, one Light Recovery Section and one Ordnance Field Park, RAOC.

Note 3. At this time, one company 1 KRRC with a troop of D Bty 3 RHA formed the garrison at Siwa Oasis and the Première Compagnie d'Infanterie de Marine, the vanguard of the Free French Forces of the Western Desert, was serving with the Support Group.

Cunningham. Operation Crusader would be launched on the 16th, with XXX Corps circumventing Rommel's forces, threatening his supply lines and forcing him to expend his armour in a high-attrition attack on the massed guns of 7th Armd Division in a preselected killing ground. Meanwhile, XIII Corps would move down the coast to relieve Tobruk.

Initially the plan went so well that Rommel had no idea he had been outflanked, but the British armour then divided itself in various directions, each brigade lacking the

Below left and Below: Operation Crusader, 16 November–15 December. 1 — the British advance toward Sidi Rezegh, outflanking Rommel on 18–21 November; 2 — the Tobruk Garrison joins the attack; 22–23 November. (See page 24 for map 3.)

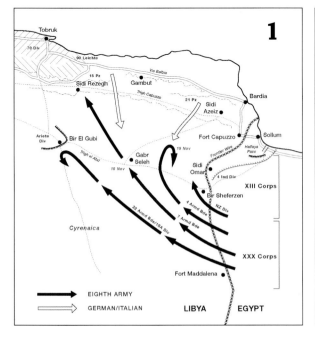
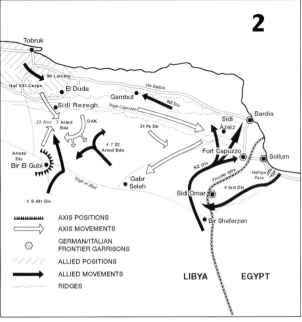

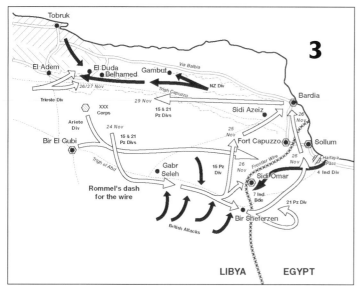

3

LIBYA EGYPT

Above: Operation Crusader 16 November–15 December. 3 — the German attacks of 24 November onward.

Below: Spoils of war 2. Another "capture" by the Cherry Pickers armoured cars was this umbrella — possibly from the famous "Groppis" nightclub in Cairo. The Morris CS9/LAC was acting as regimental rear link at Bir Sheferzen, July 1940.

strength to accomplish its individual tasks. No wonder Rommel so often remarked: "What does it matter if you have two tanks to my one, when you spread them out and let me smash them in detail?"

4th Armd Bde, having drifted east to protect the flank of XIII Corps, was attacked by first one, and then by both, Panzer divisions, which then turned north together. 7th Armd Bde, followed by the Support Group, then went north to what was to become the main battle area, namely the airfield at Sidi Rezegh, just south of Tobruk. They occupied the town and airfield, but could not take the dominant surrounding hills. The two Panzer divisions then fell on the 7th Bde from the south, inflicting severe losses.

22nd Armd went west to attack the Italian Ariete Division, and had soon overrun the Italians at Gubi. However, owing to the lack of infantry support, it could not hold its gains and was then switched, initially to help the other two armoured brigades as the battle built up at Sidi Rezegh.

Despite its gallant efforts and those of the Tobruk garrison to break out, the division never managed to achieve sufficient decisive strength at the critical point of impact and on 22 November the Support Group was driven off the airfield by determined enemy counterattacks. During the two days of unceasing battle, in which it had stubbornly held out, the Support Group had been awarded no less than three Victoria Crosses (see pages 84–5 for full citations). Two were posthumous — Rifleman J. Beeley of the KRRC died while charging a machine-gun nest and Lt Ward Gunn, RHA, was killed while firing a 2pdr anti-tank gun from a burning portee. The third VC was awarded to Brig "Jock" Campbell, who organised and led many armoured counter-attacks in his open-topped, unarmoured staff car, holding the defence together by his stalwart example.

The Battle Damage Assessment for 24 November revealed the severity of the impact on the division — 4th Armd Bde's HQ and 8th Hussars had both been virtually wiped out, 22nd Armd Bde reduced to a single composite regiment and 7th Armd Bde had virtually ceased to exist. Rommel, thinking that XXX Corps was finished, raced eastwards towards the frontier to take on XIII Corps. However, despite having dominated Gen Cunningham (who was replaced by Auchinleck with Lt-Gen Ritchie), he had reacted too late. XIII Corps was progressing well down the coast and eventually recaptured Sidi Rezegh and even managed to link up briefly with the Tobruk garrison.

Taking advantage of this breathing space in the battle, 7 Armd Div was now able to reorganise and achieve some resupply of new tanks as well as salvage many others from the battlefield. When the Panzers returned to the west on 27 November to aid other Axis troops around Tobruk, 4th and 22nd Brigades had amassed 120 tanks between them and attacked a

weakened 15th Panzer Division which they managed to catch on its own. However, its own intrinsic supporting arms of artillery and infantry enabled it to hold off the two brigades until nightfall, when it broke off contact.

XIII Corps was then forced to give up Sidi Rezegh as the Germans broke back through its positions and also cut the tenuous link established with Tobruk, while XXX Corps was held off to the south and prevented from coming to its aid.

By this time, however, attrition had also taken its toll on the Germans, who were forced to abandon their remaining frontier defences and pull back first to Gazala and finally by the end of the year to Agheila, the British taking Benghazi on 25 December.

Operation Crusader was the thus fastest moving, farthest ranging and most complex battle of the whole desert war. It was also perhaps 7 Armd Div's finest hour, when, despite inferior equipment and high attrition, it took a heavy toll of the *Afrika Korps* and won three VCs for outstanding bravery.

ACTION IN THE FAR EAST

Now action in other parts of the world would have its effect on the war in the desert. Japan's unprovoked attack on Pearl Harbor on 7 December 1941, coupled with Japanese assaults on Hong Kong, Singapore, Malaya and then Burma, meant that once again units destined for the Middle East Command, or already serving there, had to be transferred to the Far East. These included 7th Armoured Brigade, who, having changed its "Red Rat" symbol for a "Green Rat", carried out a masterly withdrawal through Burma, covering the retreating British forces safely back into India. In addition, the disastrous fall of Greece was followed swiftly by the successful German airborne assault on Crete, leaving the tiny but now vitally important island of Malta virtually unprotected. The brave population and its small garrison were subjected to the full weight of Axis air attacks, as they endeavoured to bomb the Maltese into submission. Fortunately they did not succeed. However, Axis resupply to North Africa was able to be stepped up, their convoys gaining increased protection from both U-boats and surface vessels as well as from the air. Axis influence in the Mediterranean was now at its height, enabling Rommel to receive replenishment and to plan, then launch, a fresh offensive.

Below: Getting to grips with their "Honeys". 5 RTR tank crewmen learning all about their new Light tanks, which they are just drawing up from Ordnance. They are looking carefully at the excellent .30 Browning light machine gun, the standard MG on American tanks throughout the war that is still in service worldwide.

After Operation Crusader, 7th Armoured Division had been taken out of the line to undergo another period of rest and refit, which included major changes to the divisional organisation. The division was reorganised into two armoured brigades and one lorried infantry brigade, with the main elements of the Support Group being divided between the three, so that all had, for example, integral artillery and Engineer support. In addition, the division received new tanks, generously provided by America — first the M3 Light Stuart, which, although only equipped with a 37mm main gun, was infinitely superior to the current British light tank in service. Next came the M3 Medium Grant with its thicker armour and 75mm gun, which was

Above: More newly issued "Honeys" are given a close examination by these 5 RTR officers. Note the "A" Squadron triangle on the turret and the 7th Armd Div "Desert Rat" on the nearest mudguard.

Above right: This replenishment point at Bir Sherferzen is a hive of activity as men of 1 RB replenish from cans — both the flimsy British 2-gallon can and the more durable German 4.5-gallon (20-litre) "Jerricans" are in evidence. Water was carried in much the same cans, so they had to be carefully marked to prevent mistakes — eg water cans were always black with "WATER" stencilled on them in white. Also, the 7th Armd Div sign is just visible on the tailboard of one of the 15cwt trucks.

Right: After the battle of Alam Halfa 30 August– 7 September 1942. The Germans seemed in control and Suez was threatened.

far superior to the British cruisers of the period and had a devastating effect on German armour when it first saw action. Each armoured regiment now had 24 Grants and 20 Stuarts. Also the 2pdr anti-tank gun began to be replaced by the far superior 6pdr, which went some way to restoring the balance against the German anti-tank guns, although none was comparable with the lethality of the 88mm. At this time the division tragically lost its newly appointed GOC, Maj-Gen "Jock" Campbell VC, killed in a freak driving accident. Campbell had just taken over from Gen "Strafer" Gott, who had himself been promoted to corps commander, then selected as the future Eighth Army commander, only to be killed when his aircraft was shot down whilst flying back to Cairo. Maj-Gen Frank Messervy of 4th Ind Div took over as divisional commander.

GAZALA

At the beginning of April 1942 the division returned to the desert as part of a defensive line, stretching from Gazala south to Bir Hacheim. It was made up of a series of fortified "boxes", protected by minefields. Churchill continually exhorted Gen Ritchie to go on the offensive, but, before he could do so, Rommel again seized the initiative and attacked first, retaking Agedabia. Originally planned as only another pre-emptive spoiling attack, his initial success spurred him on and on 26 May he launched Operation Venezia, skirting south of Bir Hacheim and then swinging north/northeast in a compact spearhead containing his main armoured formations. He caught 4th Armd Bde dispersed and vulnerable, overwhelming a major portion of its armour and throwing the rest into confusion. On 27 May Gen Messervy and his HQ were overrun and captured, although he later managed to disguise himself as a private soldier, then to escape and reassume command of his division.

The German assault was eventually checked by 1st Armd Div, whose Grants and 6pdr anti-tank guns came as a shock to Rommel, who now found himself in a critical position, virtually surrounded by minefields and "boxes". This phase of the battle, known as the "Cauldron", once again illustrates the superior enemy use of his all-arms organisation and equipment, for when the British attacked the "Cauldron" piecemeal they incurred heavy losses. Rommel then broke out and, clearing safe lanes through the minefields, took the critical 150th Brigade box. He then rolled up the line, taking box after box, the British having no choice but to fall back in a fighting withdrawal, with delaying actions near Sidi Rezegh and Mersa Matruh. They were pushed back to the Alamein-Ruweisat Ridge area. Tobruk had finally fallen on 21 June and Allied fortunes were at their lowest ebb — Rommel having been promoted to Field Marshal by Adolf Hitler for his successes. Cairo and the Suez Canal now appeared to be his for the taking.

However, the Germans were actually at the end of their tether. Behind them stretched mile upon mile of tortuous supply lines, whilst the British, despite having their "backs to the wall", were never closer to their own supply dumps. They also now had a new army commander, the charismatic Gen Bernard Law Montgomery, who would prove equal to the traumatic situation in which the Eighth Army now found itself. He ordered "No Withdrawal" and then made certain that his troops were in strong defensive positions at Alam al Halfa and had the wherewithal to defend themselves. In the July battles that followed, 7th Armoured met the enemy armour, checked it and destroyed many enemy tanks, forcing Rommel back on the defensive.

A rejuvenated Eighth Army now prepared for what would prove to be the most important battle of the Desert War. However, unlike his predecessors, "Monty" refused to be rushed into battle, carefully building up his supplies, manpower and weapons — which now included quantities of the even more powerful, reliable and manoeuvrable M4 Medium Sherman tank, the successor to the Grant. By the time it was ready for battle in mid-

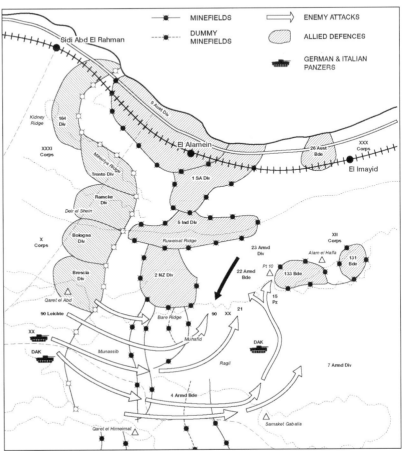

"Danger! Fitters at work!" It's amazing how innovative fitters can be. In the first picture (**Opposite, Above**) they are using a German 88mm AA/Anti-tank gun as a crane, to lift the gun out of what appears to be a German eight-wheeled armoured car. In the second (**Opposite, Below**) a fitter works on the radial engine of a Grant Medium tank (note the "Desert Rat" sign on the rear) whilst the crew members have a kip in their bivvie alongside the tank. The third shot (**Above**) shows a tank transporter crew, having loaded a cruiser tank, struggling to load one of the girders it has used to get the tank on board. Finally (**Left**), at the rear of what appears to be a tank open leaguer on either side of the coast road, another tank transporter, with a Sherman on its trailer, prepares to move off. Fitters on both sides did a marvellous job of keeping the tanks fit and ready for action.

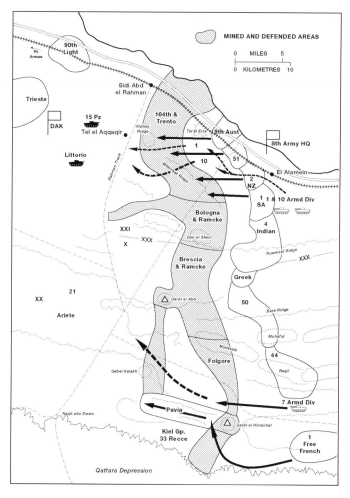

MINED AND DEFENDED AREAS

0 MILES 5

0 KILOMETRES 10

October, Montgomery's army easily outnumbered Rommel's, although the Axis forces were in a strong defensive position astride the El Alamein feature, protected by vast minefields (Rommel's "Devil's Gardens") and in-depth positions.

7th Armoured Division's initial task in the battle was to contain 21st Panzer Division in the south. It began by penetrating the first minefield, then forming a bridgehead, but progress was slow and by 27 October Montgomery had decided not to continue the main thrust there, but rather to look for an easier spot nearer the coast. 7th Armoured was accordingly moved north, then went into reserve as the infantry divisions pounded away. A few days later (2 November) it managed to make its way forward south of Tel el Eisa, ready to exploit any breakthrough. This took place shortly afterwards, the division being heavily engaged by enemy armour south of Tel el Aqqaqir. Here it destroyed 19 enemy tanks and forced the enemy to withdraw. This proved to be the beginning of the pursuit, although initially unexpectedly heavy rain saturated the ground and made the going virtually impossible, thus allowing the enemy to escape. Led by its armoured car regiment, the ubiquitous 11th Hussars, the division finally managed to break out through the remaining enemy positions to the west and after a short fight finished off the stubborn German and Italian rearguards, crossing the Egyptian frontier for a final time on the 9th. Further bad weather and petrol shortages continued to delay the advance, until the port facilities in Tobruk could be put back into service.

Above: The turn of the tide — the battle of El Alamein 22 October–4 November 1942.

Right: The divisional organisation as at October 1942.

Above right: Although radios were used for long-distance communications, land line was still laid on occasions, such as here at Agedabia, at a time when the battle was fairly static for a while.

Centre right: Despatch riders were also used to carry messages, such as this signalman (Jeff Orchard) on his beloved Norton motorcycle. Nortons were widely used, over 100,000 being produced during the war, the 16H being built in the greatest quantity.

Bottom right: The Afrike Korps retreats — El Alamein to Tunis, October 1942 to May 1943 — showing the route taken by 7th Armoured.

7th Armoured Division HQ		
4th Light Armoured Brigade	**22nd Armoured Brigade**	**131st (Queen's) Brigade**
3 RHA	1 RTR	1/5 Queen's
R Scots Greys	5 RTR	1/6 Queen's
4 H + sqn 8 H	4 CLY	1/7 Queen's
2 Derbys Yeo	4 Fd Regt, RA	53 Fd Regt, RA
1 KRRC	97 Fd Regt, RA	2 x btys 57 Atk Regt, RA
	1 RB	11 Fd Coy RE
Divisional Troops		
11 H		
15 LAA Regt, RA		
65 Atk Regt, RA		
(Norfolk Yeo)		
Div Sigs		
4th and 21 Fd Sqn, RE		
143 Fd Pk Sqn, RE		
5, 10, 58, 67, 287, 432 and 507 Coys RASC		Note 1. Also one OFP and
2, 7, 14 and 15 Lt Fd Amb RAMC		one Wksp RAOC per
Div OFP and 15 LAA Wksp RAOC		Brigade

THE WITHDRAWAL

Slowly but surely, the Axis forces were pushed back until they reached strong positions astride the Tripoli road at Tarhuna. However, these did not hold for long and on 23 January 1943, the "Desert Rats" entered Tripoli unopposed. The ailing *Afrika Korps* fought on with its usual tenacity, causing numerous casualties through mines, boobytraps and rearguard ambushes. Just before reaching Tripoli, the Divisional commander, Gen John Harding, had been badly wounded by shellfire. He was replaced by Gen Bobbie Erskine who would lead the Division on to the Mareth Line and for the rest of its time in North Africa, then on into Italy and Northwest

Europe, the second longest period in command of any 7th Armoured GOC. On 6 March came Rommel's first major counteroffensive which culminated in the Battle of Medenine. Here, the enemy for once was forced into making an ill-judged attack against strong, well-prepared positions, where the division's tanks and anti-tank guns were firmly located. The anti-tank guns, especially those of the Queen's Brigade, caused heavy casualties.

The division played only a small part in the subsequent battles of Mareth and Wadi Akarit, but was first into Sfax on 10 April. During the battle of Enfidaville, the division was suddenly switched (making a 300-mile journey on tank transporters) from the Eighth to the First Army, in order to attack from Medjez in the west towards Tunis and then to wheel north to link up with the Americans. On 6 May, two infantry divisions followed by two armoured divisions, one being 7th Armoured, all under the command of Gen Horrocks, with heavy artillery and air support, smashed their way through to Tunis in a highly successful "textbook" operation — a rewarding note on which to end a gruelling campaign.

After 2,000 miles and six months' hard fighting from Alamein to Tunis, in which the division had played so great a part, the Allies had succeeded in completely destroying the Axis forces and expelling them from North Africa. It was now time for a well-earned rest, before embarking on the invasion of Italy.

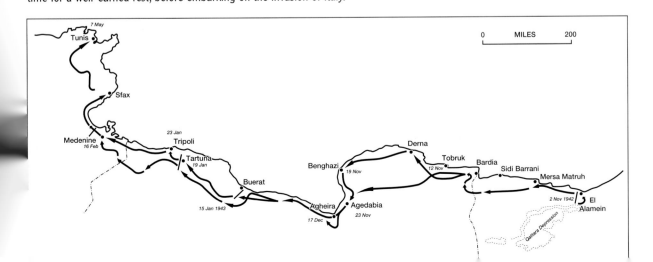

Right: "Fighting fit and fit to fight!" Whilst preparing for El Alamein, everyone had to undergo some tough training. This photo of how to deal with a sentry was on the front of the *Tough Tactics* pamphlet, the brainchild of Maj (later Lt-Col) Jerry Hedley of 7th Armd Div.

Below: Montgomery's Message to his Troops on the Eve of the Battle of El Alamein. "Monty" was a great one for getting his message down to every private soldier and issued communiqués like this one before each important event and battle.

EIGHTH ARMY

Personal Message from the ARMY COMMANDER

1—When I assumed command of the Eighth Army I said that the mandate was to destroy ROMMEL and his Army, and that it would be done as soon as we were ready.

2—We are ready NOW.

The battle which is now about to begin will be one of the decisive battles of history. It will be the turning point of the war. The eyes of the whole world will be on us, watching anxiously which way the battle will swing.

We can give them their answer at once, "It will swing our way."

3—We have first-class equipment; good tanks; good anti-tank guns; plenty of artillery and plenty of ammunition; and we are backed up by the finest air striking force in the world.

All that is necessary is that each one of us, every officer and man, should enter this battle with the determination to see it through—to fight and to kill—and finally, to win.

If we all do this there can be only one result—together we will hit the enemy for "six," right out of North Africa.

4—The sooner we win this battle, which will be the turning point of this war, the sooner we shall all get back home to our families.

5—Therefore, let every officer and man enter the battle with a stout heart, and with the determination to do his duty so long as he has breath in his body.

AND LET NO MAN SURRENDER SO LONG AS HE IS UNWOUNDED AND CAN FIGHT.

Let us all pray that "the Lord mighty in battle" will give us the victory.

B. L. MONTGOMERY,
Lieutenant-General, G.O.C.-in-C., Eighth Army.

MIDDLE EAST FORCES,
23-10-42.

Above: A Sherman burns as British tanks advance into no man's land. Although the new American M4 Medium tanks, known as the Shermans, were in many ways superior to the obsolescent British cruisers, they still caught fire very easily, earning them the unfortunate nickname "The Ronson Lighter", as they were guaranteed to light first time. The Germans called them "Tommy Cookers" for the same reason.

Left: El Alamein: the long retreat begins. On the other side of the minefields, after a stubborn defence, Field Marshal Erwin Rommel, the "Desert Fox" and his *Afrika Korps*, had to begin a long, painful withdrawal that would end up with the Axis troops surrendering in Tunis. However, they conducted it extremely tenaciously and never allowed it to become a rout.

Opposite, Below: El Alamein. Lit by the eerie light of the massive artillery barrage, Sappers begin the difficult and dangerous job of gapping the German minefields — Rommel's "Devil's Gardens" as they were called. They used mine detectors to locate the mines, then they had to prod for them with their bayonets and finally lift them by hand.

Right: Tobruk recaptured. Men of the 1/6 Queen's enter Tobruk. After two sieges and many battles, the little port was at last in British hands for good and all! As seen here, even in an armoured division the infantry had to march quite a lot of the time.

Below: Victory parade in Tripoli. The Prime Minister, Mr Winston Churchill, passing through the main street in Tripoli inspecting the victorious troops. To his rear are the Crusader tanks of C Sqn 4 CLY. The A15 Crusader was the best of the early cruisers, much superior to the others although still armed with only a 2pdr gun as its main armament. However, the final production version, the Mark III, had a 6pdr plus additional armour on its hull and turret. *IWM — E22280*

Inset: On to Tunis! Stirring headlines of the *Tripoli Times* for 23 March 1943 as the 8th Army joins with the 1st Army on the last lap through Tunisia.

Left: The first British troops into Tripoli were the members of this 11th Hussars armoured car crew, commanded by Sgt Hugh Lyon. Having been first into both Tobruk and Benghazi, the "Cherry Pickers" could rightfully claim the triple crown, albeit if only by a short head from the troops advancing along the coast road!

Below: Whilst King George VI was visiting the division he inspected the "Cherry Pickers" on 21 June. He is seen here accompanied by the CO of 11 H, Lt-Col Smail, plus the Army commander ("Monty") and the GOC (Erskine). HM The King was their Colonel-in-Chief.

7th Armoured Division HQ

22nd Armoured Brigade	Divisional Troops
1RTR	11H
5RTR	Div Sigs
4CLY	3RHA
1RB	5RHA
	15 LAA Regt, RA
	24 Fd Regt, RA
	65 Atk Regt (Nor Yeo)
131st (Queen's) Brigade	69 Med Regt, RA
1/5 Queen's	146 Fd Regt, RA
1/6 Queen's	4 and 621 Fd Sqn, 143 Fd Pk Sqn, RE
1/7 Queen's	5, 58, 67, 287, 432 and 507 Coys RASC
C Coy 1 Cheshire (MMG)	2 and 131 Fd Amb, 70 Fd Hygiene Sect, 21
	Mobile CCS, 3 FSU, 7 Fd Transfusion Unit,
	132 and 135 Mobile Dental Units RAMC
	Div OFP RAOC
	22 Armd Bde Wksp
	131 Bde Wksp
	15 LAA Wksp

Top: Organisation of the division in September 1943 (while in Italy).

Above: Loading for Italy: one of the ACVs belonging to the division being loaded for Italy. This was to follow the successful Allied amphibious landing on Sicily (Operation Husky, 10 July 1943). The British 8th Army landed on the "toe" of Italy (Operation Baytown) of 3 September, whilst the US 5th Army (which included the British 7th Armd Div) landed at Salerno (Operation Avalanche) on 9 September.

ITALY

After the surrender of the Axis forces in North Africa, instead of a wildly optimistic 2,000-mile "withdrawal", back to the fleshpots of Cairo and Alexandria, the division was extracted from Tunisia, to just along the coast of Tripolitania, for a period of relaxation, re-equipment and training. Homs, near the ancient city of Leptis Magna, was the chosen location in which it would spend the next three months. There were little signs of modern civilisation, but at least it was close to the sea, which made up for a lot and everyone swam daily. Here they prepared for a major amphibious assault on mainland Italy, as part of the US Fifth, who would take part in Operation Avalanche at Salerno on 9 September 1943. They had been left out of the earlier amphibious operation against Sicily (Operation Husky, 10 July 1943), but would soon be in the thick of it once again.

During this period there were further changes in organisation and — a tribute to the now flourishing Allied war machine — still more fresh weapons, vehicles and equipment. 22nd Armoured Brigade was brought back up to strength and was now composed almost entirely of M4 Sherman Medium tanks. 11th Hussars, the divisional armoured car regiment, was reorganised for the European theatre of operations, with an additional troop equipped with White scout cars to augment the mixed Daimler armoured car and Dingo scout car troops. The new support troop combined the roles of infantry and Engineers. The Jeep Troop was also replaced by an SP Gun Troop consisting of two 75mm SP guns, mounted in White half-tracks, to give close, immediate fire support. 5 RHA was equipped with self-propelled Priest 105mm guns, to work in close conjunction with the tanks of the armoured brigade.

The Engineers were trained to use the new Bailey bridges and tank-mounted scissors bridges for the first time. In the coming campaign they would enable the division to keep moving, by maintaining the difficult, mountainous roads in good working order and fording/bridging the various rivers and irrigation ditches which would otherwise hold up the advance at every turn.

Having landed successfully, the campaign that followed, although brief as far as the division was concerned, was complex, involving a tortuous advance into difficult terrain for the most part unsuited to armour. It was a mountainous area with fierce rivers and bad roads, which in wet weather could hold up an armoured division on their own. It definitely favoured the defenders who naturally exploited the local terrain to the full. Although Italy had just surrendered, the Germans had not and, as ever, were taking their fighting seriously, opposing the Allied attacks with their usual stubbornness, under their brilliant commander Field Marshal "Smiling Albert" Kesselring. They ensured that the Allied landings, both Fifth Army at Salerno and the slightly earlier Eighth Army landing on the toe of Italy (Operation Baytown, 3 September 1943), despite Allied air superiority, were hard fought, even managing to disable a warship with a new weapon — a radio-controlled glider bomb.

7th Armoured Division had begun landing on 15 September as the follow-up division of X Corps, behind 46th and 56th Infantry Divisions who had had their work cut out for them.

The Eighth Army had made better progress further south and by 16 September the two beachheads had linked up and were pressing on northwards together, Fifth Army in the west, Eighth Army in the east. Nevertheless, the Germans fought a masterly campaign as they withdrew slowly northwards from defensive line to defensive line.

After fierce fighting, in particular by 1/7th Queen's in order to take high ground just to the south of the main road, elements of 7th Armoured covered some 50 miles in a single day and attacked Scafati on the River Sarno. Fortuitously they managed to prevent the Germans from blowing the bridge and drove them out of the town, being rapturously greeted by the inhabitants.

As the advance continued across the river, the divisional Engineers built a Bailey bridge next to the existing Scafati roadbridge, in order to relieve congestion. For the next two days (28-9 September) the divisional advance was slow but steady across countryside heavily waterlogged by recent rains and defended stubbornly with mines, booby-traps and small hardcore rearguard units. Nevertheless, on 1 October forward elements of the division entered Naples.

Beyond Naples, the country opened out and was more suited to armour which was accordingly deployed up front. For the Motor Battalion (1 RB) it was a busy and slightly frustrating time, assimilating the limitations of the new terrain which lacked the desert's freedom of manoeuvre.

By 5 October the division had reached the River Volturno near Capua, only to find that all the bridges had been blown and the enemy was strongly established on the far bank. During the following week, energetic reconnaissance by 1/7th Queen's located most of these enemy positions. Although the main Allied attack on 12 October was to be made elsewhere by the infantry, 7th Armoured was to mount its own diversionary crossing in order to keep the enemy occupied. Despite fierce opposition, 1/7th Queen's eventually managed to secure and maintain a small bridgehead into which machine guns and anti-tank guns were then ferried and hauled up the far bank by hand. Behind them the Sappers began to bridge the river. Tanks of the armoured brigade in addition managed to locate a ford where, with the aid of bulldozers and by waterproofing the tanks, they effected a crossing and began mopping up enemy positions along the bank in both directions.

Top: 7th Armoured in Italy, September – November 1943.

Above: Col Pat Hobart, the GSO1, briefs 7th Armd Div HQ personnel during the voyage to Salerno. He went on to command 1st Royal Tank Regiment, in 22nd Armd Bde, and was awarded the DSO, OBE and MC. Postwar, he reached the rank of Major-General, as Director of the Royal Armoured Corps.

For the Germans, coupled with the success of the main Allied thrust by the infantry divisions, this was just too much, so they broke off contact and withdrew to their next defence line along the River Garigliano

MONDRAGONE

The division continued to advance down the valley of the Volturno, with the Germans demolishing and destroying everything in front of them, until the division was moved further downriver towards the coast, to a marshy plain overlooked by Monte Massico. There the enemy was in a well-established position and able to observe all movement. However, careful reconnaissance revealed a possible crossing place near the river's mouth, although it had been heavily mined. At dawn on 1 November the attack went in, with the mines cleared and 5 RTR making a successful crossing, while 1/6th Queen's attacked Mondragone further upriver, taking first the village and then going on to dislodge the enemy from his commanding ridge positions and to occupy the whole mountain. 1RTR then took Cicola after a brief but intense battle and the 22nd Armd Bde moved up to Sessa Aurunca to join up with 46th Division. This would be the division's last operation in Italy.

By 19 November, the division had been withdrawn back behind Monte Massico near the Volturno once more and an advance party had already set sail — destination England. The "Desert Rats", as one of the most experienced formations of the British Army, had been chosen to take part in the coming Allied invasion of Normandy. Having handed all their tanks and equipment over to the Canadian 5th Armoured Division, they made their way back to the docks in Naples, boarded troop transports, and reached the UK on 7 January 1944.

Above: Tanks of 5 RTR in the square at Sparanise, having cleared the surrounding area in late October 1943. The division's time in Italy was now almost over, as "Monty" had chosen it to be among the seasoned troops to return to the UK for the Normandy landings.

Above left: First sight of Italy, evening of 8 September 1943. The assault was led by British 46th Inf Div and 56th (London) Armoured Division of X Corps, with 7th Armoured Division as the follow-up force. They had heard the announcement that the Italians had surrendered and many thought the landing would be unopposed, but the Germans swiftly disarmed the Italians and took over their positions, so the assault was met with well-controlled enemy fire.

Left: Crossing the Volturno, 7 to 16 October 1943. The division first had to carry out an assault river crossing, establish a firm bridgehead in the area of the village of Grazzanise, then the Sappers were able to construct bridges over the fast-flowing river

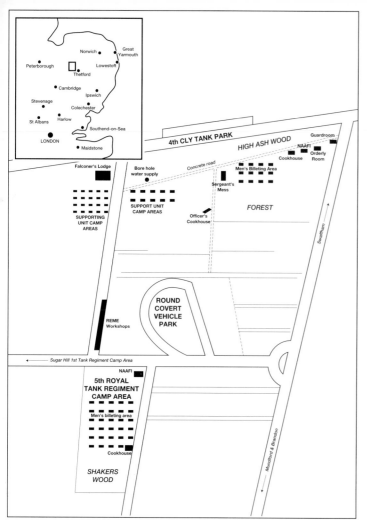

Map labels:
Great Yarmouth
Norwich
Peterborough
Lowestoft
Thetford
Cambridge
Ipswich
Stevenage
Colechester
St Albans
Harlow
Southend-on-Sea
LONDON
Maidstone

4th CLY TANK PARK
HIGH ASH WOOD
Guardroom
NAAFI
Orderly Room
Cookhouse
Falconer's Lodge
Bore hole water supply
Concrete road
Men's Billeting Area
Sergeant's Mess
SUPPORT UNIT CAMP AREAS
FOREST
SUPPORTING UNIT CAMP AREAS
Officer's Cookhouse
Swaffham
REME Workshops
ROUND COVERT VEHICLE PARK
Sugar Hill 1st Tank Regiment Camp Area
NAAFI
5th ROYAL TANK REGIMENT CAMP AREA
Men's billeting area
Mundford & Brandon
Cookhouse
SHAKERS WOOD

Above: Preparing for Normandy — 7th Armoured in the Thetford area, December 1943 to June 1944.

CONCENTRATION AND REORGANISATION IN BLIGHTY

After its well-deserved disembarkation leave, the division assembled in its allocated concentration area in Norfolk. The Queen's Brigade got the better choice of billets, being mainly quartered in "civilisation" around King's Lynn. 22nd Armoured Brigade units on the other hand were in the damp Thetford forests near Brandon, occupying "… groups of decayed Nissen huts clustered beneath tall pines". The 4 CLY camp was probably the worst of all, being both cold and wet, having been constructed well below the water level, whilst any form of heating was severely rationed! Here the division received its quota of new recruits to make units up to strength, whilst many of its old hands were cross-posted to other formations to give them a leavening of battle experience — in this way the "Desert Rats" lost the commander of their lorried infantry brigade, the senior staff officer of the division and the Chief Signals Officer. Many members of the division had been fighting since Italy first declared war in June 1940 and had been through both the entire North African campaign and Italy. Some of these old hands undoubtedly felt it was time that somebody else "had a go" and vocally expressed this opinion. This meant that the GOC, Gen Bobbie Erskine, had to pay considerable attention to the maintenance of morale during this preparatory period. The situation wasn't helped by the fact that, before pre-invasion training could be started, a complete scale of new equipment for the entire division had to be drawn up. This in itself was a major undertaking and it did not make matters any easier to discover that the armoured regiments were to be equipped with an entirely new cruiser tank — the A27M Cromwell. Fast (except in reverse gear), with a reliable Rolls-Royce engine, it was however thinly armoured and, with a 75mm main armament, undergunned. Many considered it, with justification, to be inferior to their well-loved Shermans. Erskine wrote: "We knew the Sherman inside out, but none of us knew the Cromwell — many of which suffered from minor defects, and the reputation of the tank did not improve as we had to repair the defects ourselves. The armoured regiments all had to go to Scotland (Kirkcudbright) to do their gunnery which was absolutely necessary, but took up much time on a form of training which could have been avoided if we had been given Shermans … We left for Normandy with a high state of morale, but it is no use concealing the fact that we felt we had been rushed. We were nothing like so well teamed up as we had been before Salerno."

Fortunately, alongside the Cromwells, each troop was issued with a Sherman Firefly, a British-modified Sherman mounting a 17pdr main gun which was one of the most effective Allied tank guns of the war. The divisional armoured car regiment (11 H) temporarily became corps troops, but later returned to under divisional control in Normandy, providing, as always, invaluable medium reconnaissance. Additionally, there was the divisional close reconnaissance regiment, the 8th Hussars, which had the same equipment (Cromwells and Stuarts) as the armoured regiments of 22nd Armoured Brigade. As a result, it tended to be used as a fourth armoured regiment, being allocated

7th Armoured Division HQ

22nd Armoured Brigade
1 RTR
5 RTR
4 CLY (until Jul 1944)
5 RIDG (from Jul 1944)

131st (Queen's) Brigade
(1)
1/5 Queen's
1/6 Queen's
1/7 Queen's
No 3 Sp Coy RNF

Divisional Troops
8 H
11 H
Div Sigs

Divisional Artillery
3 RHA
5 RHA
15 LAA RA
65 Atk Regt RA
(Norfolk Yeo)

Medical
2 Lt Fd Amb RAMC
131 Fd Amb
29 FDS
70 Fd Hygiene Sect
134 Mob Dental Unit

Divisional Engineers
4 Fd Sqn
621 Fd Sqn
143 Fd Pk Sqn

EME
7 Armd Tps Wksp
22 Armd Bde Wksp
131 Bde Wksp
15 LAA Wksp

Divisional S&T
No 58 Coy RASC
No 67 Coy RASC
No 507 Coy RASC
No 133 Coy RASC (2)

Ordnance
Div OFP
22 Armd Bde OFP
131 Bde OFP

RAC
No 263 Fwd Del Sqn

Note 1. From Nov 1944 131 Bde comprised 1/5 Queen's, 2nd Devons and 9 DLI plus No 3 Sp Coy RNF.

Note 2. From Jan 1945

Left: Organisation of the division on 6 July.

Below: Handing over to the Canadians. 22nd Armd Bde workshops in the middle of its handover to its Canadian counterparts in 5th Canadian Armoured Division — conducted in a sea of mud! The brigade had to leave its Sherman tanks in Italy and would be re-equipped with Cromwells when it reached England.

The divisional artillery contained both towed and self-propelled guns, whilst the divisional anti-tank regiment (Norfolk Yeomanry) had two batteries of self-propelled 17pdrs, the rest being towed, first by half-tracks and later by converted Crusader tanks. Amongst the supporting services, the REME had been massively expanded, now having separate workshops for each brigade and divisional troops, along with Centaur or Cromwell armoured recovery vehicles, whilst the Sappers had "scissors" and Bailey bridges. Divisional communications had been considerably improved with the issue of new radio equipment based on the WS19.

As can be seen from these examples, Allied equipment procurement was running at full spate as everyone prepared for D-Day The division was now a fully functioning all-arms formation, with a high level of "on call" air support. Nevertheless, the coming campaign would be another gruelling, hard-fought struggle against a determined enemy who had, despite shrinking resources, upgraded much of his own equipment. Throughout the war the Germans had led the field in tank design and their Tiger and Panther heavy tanks, though still somewhat mechanically unreliable, were massively better armoured and

Below: Gen Montgomery inspected every unit in the division on 16 and 17 February 1944. Here he inspects 4 CLY, now one of the armoured regiments in 22nd Armd Bde. He made a point of giving each unit a rousing speech. *IWM — H36004*

nned than their Allied counterparts. Opposing the "Desert Rats" in Normandy was their d desert adversary — Field Marshal Erwin Rommel, the "Desert Fox" himself, who now, the commander of Army Group "B", had done much to bolster the "Atlantic Wall" efences. Another important figure from the division's past actively commanding a ontline formation in Normandy was its creator, Gen Percy Hobart. After raising and aining both 7th and 11th Armoured Divisions, he had gone on to create the evolutionary "Funnies" (79th Armd Div), whose specialised vehicles such as swimming nks, flamethrowers, mineclearers and all manner of mobile bridges, Engineer vehicles c would play such a major part on the British and Canadian beaches in overcoming of e enemy's defences.

A few weeks before D-Day everyone moved even deeper into the fir woods and camps ere sealed, the soldiers spending most of their time waterproofing their vehicles. ventually, the units moved down to their embarkation points — boarding the LSTs in number of different places, then collecting into a convoy off Deal on the afternoon and vening of 5 June. By the evening of D-Day they had crossed the Channel and were in e vicinity of the landing beaches, but did not actually start to land until about 1100 ours on the 7th.

NORMANDY

th Armoured Division landed successfully in France on 7 June after being delayed by ad weather. Fortunately, however, only a few vehicles were lost in the surf, and by that vening 22nd Armoured Brigade, less 1 RB, was safely in its oncentration area. The following morning it was ready to upport what were in the main, initially anyway, infantry perations. 5 RTR was first into action, supporting 56th Brigade n dealing with stubborn pockets of enemy at Sully and Port en Bessin. It would soon be involved in very different fighting in he thick bocage country of Normandy to what it had been used o in the Western Desert or even Italy. Now commanders were ulnerable at close-range from enemy snipers, whilst bypassed mall groups of enemy were able to knock out AFVs with close-ange, handheld anti-tank weapons such as the *Panzerfaust* the German equivalent of the PIAT or Bazooka) — so death urked around every corner.

The overall XXX Corps plan, Operation Perch, was that, aving landed on Gold Beach, 50th Infantry Division would apture Bayeux, secure the road from there to Tilly sur Seulles, hen break through the enemy positions in the area of Tilly, uvigny, Hottot and la Senaudiere. The initial attacks would be upported by naval gunfire as well as close air support. Once he way was clear then 7th Armoured would pass through, take Villers Bocage en route, then press on to the important high ground around Evrecy. This last manoeuvre was to be supported by an airborne landing (codenamed Wild Oats). Having secured a firm base in the "Suisse Normande", the armour would then turn eastwards towards Thury Harcourt and the Orne River crossings.

Unfortunately, the airborne part of the operation never came to fruition, whilst 50th Infantry Division, after taking Bayeux

Below: France 7 June – September 1944 including Villers Bocage 12–14 June.

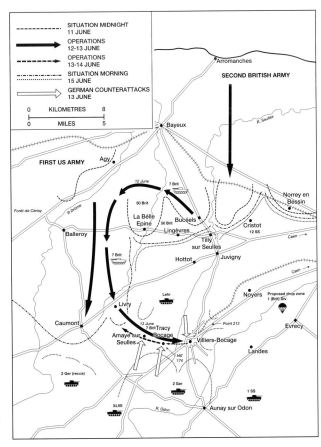

Left: Two of these three senior commanders helped to control the destiny of 7th Armd Div in the early days in Normandy. They were, left to right: Lt-Gen J. T. Crocker, GOC I Corps, Lt-Gen M. C. Dempsey GOC British 2nd Army and Lt-Gen G. C. Bucknall, GOC XXX Corps, in which 7th Armd Div served. Bucknall would be "sacked" by "Monty" after the Villers Bocage debacle. *IWM — B5326*

Below left: Into the bocage. A column of vehicles led by a Cromwell of 4 CLY moves down an unmade up road, to the south of Bayeux, as part of the "right hook" towards Villers Bocage. The patchwork of small fields, thick hedgerows and sunken roads, made the bocage ideal country for the defence.

Opposite, Above: Normandy. The division was not employed on D-Day, but landed on Gold Beach on 7 June. This photograph was taken during the journey across the Channel and shows some of the vast armada of ships sailing across the Channel.

Opposite, Below: A Crusader AA tank, belonging to 4 CLY, leaves the massive doors of the LST and makes its way ashore through the surf. There were three versions of AA Crusaders: the MkI with a single 40mm Bofors, the MkII with twin Oerlikons (as in the photo) and a few with triple Oerlikons. *IWM — B5129*

without too much trouble, got itself bogged down in its attack in the Tilly sur Seulles area, due mainly to the close, difficult, bocage countryside. Lack of progress led Montgomery to decide to modify his strategy and to send 7th Armoured on a daring "right hook" to capture Villers Bocage and the high ground to its northeast, then to push on to Evrecy.

Initially, all went well and, by 0900 hours 13 June, the division's advance guard (A Sqn 4 CLY/A Coy 1 RB) had motored virtually unhindered through Villers Bocage and reached the high ground to its northeast (Point 213). Unbeknown to it, however, part of 2 Kompanie, schwere SS-Panzer Abteilung 101, under the command of the redoubtable Panzer ace, Obersturmführer Michael Wittmann, was already leaguered there and, before 4 CLY could react, his heavy Tiger tanks created havoc among the lighter, underarmoured and undergunned Cromwells, Stuarts and half-tracks of the British force. In the ensuing battle Wittmann and his Tigers knocked out or captured the majority of the advance guard, before Wittmann's vehicle was itself knocked out and he had to escape on foot. After a fierce battle, 22nd Armd Bde Group withdrew from the little

Left: Devastation at Villers Bocage. This is one of the 4 CLY Cromwells that was knocked out by Michael Wittmann and his Tiger tank as it swept down the advance guard column from Point 213 and into the village. The tank belonged to Capt Paddy Victory. *IWM — B 8633*

Below left: Cromwell tanks and M10 tank destroyers of 22 Armd Bde in an open leaguer in their concentration area just before an attack east of the Orne River, July 1944. The M10 was an open-topped tank destroyer, mounting a 3in gun, that was based upon the Sherman hull. A British version, known as "Achilles", mounted a 17pdr, was only in service in limited numbers, but was highly successful.

Below: Two officers of 5th Inniskilling Dragoon Guards, the regiment which replaced 4 CLY in 22 Armd Bde after Villers Bocage (4 CLY was amalgamated with its sister regiment 3 CLY), inspect a knocked out German PzKpfw V Panther tank. This heavy Medium tank was one of the best produced by the Germans and owes much of its design to the Soviet T34. It was knocked out by C Sqn of the "Skins" south of Canville whilst attacking Mont Pincon, 14 August 1944.

Above: Obviously a vintage year! A "Skins" crew enjoying a local bottle of wine. 5 Innis DG quickly settled into 22 Armd Bde, with 1st and 5th RTR. The brigade would remain unchanged for the rest of the war.

town into a "brigade box" to the northwest, near Amaye dur Seulles, where it successfully held off enemy attacks that night and the next morning, until being withdrawn, after inflicting considerable casualties on the enemy.

The Villers Bocage battle would have considerable long-term effects on the division. For example, the weakened 4 CLY was some weeks later (30 July) combined with 3 CLY to form a single regiment and left 7th Armoured Division, their place being taken by the 5th Royal Inniskilling Dragoon Guards (5 DG). Additionally, the XXX Corps commander, Lt-Gen Bucknall, the divisional commander, Maj-Gen Erskine, 22nd Armd Bde commander, the eccentric Brig "Looney" Hinde, and the divisional CRA, Brig R Mews, were all "sacked" by "Monty". Maj-Gen G. L. Verney, a "no-nonsense" Guardsman, took over as GOC, whilst the popular and capable Lt-Gen Brian Horrocks once again became corps commander. These changes did not, however, actually take effect until late July.

For the rest of the month the division held the line a couple of miles from Caumont, running through Bricquessard and Torteval, with an ever-growing casualty list from being under continuous attack and shelling. Eventually it handed over to the American 2nd Armd Div at the end of the month, going to the rear for rest and refit. During three weeks of fighting in Normandy the division had lost 1,149 all ranks.

OPERATION GOODWOOD

The next operation was Goodwood — an attack by VIII Corps (now commanded by ex-WDF commander and escaped POW Gen Sir Richard O'Connor) to the south east from

Caen consisting of three British armoured divisions — 7th, 11th and the Guards Armoured. The express purpose of this action was to engage as much German armour and resources as possible in the area, thus helping the Americans to break out in the west (Operation Cobra). The countryside was more open than the bocage but there were a couple ridges and several railway embankments that were impassable for tanks, which meant that the deployment of the three armoured divisions over the Orne was an extremely complicated operation. The attack was preceded by a massive aerial and artillery bombardment. The armour began to advance on 18 July with the three armoured regiments of 11th Armd Div leading. Initially, the Germans were stunned after the massive bombardment, but gradually resistance stiffened, and at Cagny the attack was held all day. Slowly the division moved forward, fighting bitterly for every village and ridge — Le Poirier, Four, Soliers, Bras, Hubert-Folie, la Hogue. By the end of the day, divisional losses were substantial in both men and armour. However, in the morning the advance was resumed, but resistance became even stronger. On 20 July, 5 RTR took Bourguebus and 4 CLY cut the Caen-Falaise road, when massive rainstorms then brought all further operations to a halt. The division was now bunched up and within enemy artillery range, so suffered accordingly, even undergoing visits from enemy reconnaissance planes, then bombers. As much support as possible was given to the division from RAF rocket-firing Typhoons.

OPERATION SPRING

On 25 July, 7th Armd Div was ordered to support 2nd and 3rd Canadian Divisions in their assault on May-sur-Orne and Tilly-la-Compagne respectively. The May-sur-Orne attack started well but was heavily counterattacked in the evening and although this was repulsed, the use of hull-down enemy armour on the overlooking ridge made things very uncomfortable. The Tilly attack also ran into fierce resistance, however the aim of the operation had been successful — the enemy had been required to bring in reserves from all over to deal with what it thought was the main Allied thrust, consequently, the American Cobra breakout on the 25th was materially assisted. From 26 to 28 July the division remained in a defensive position supporting the Canadians, then was ordered to join XXX Corps in the Caumont sector.

FRANCE AND THE LOW COUNTRIES

In order to continue to take pressure off Cobra, "Monty" launched Operation Bluecoat, using both VIII and XXX Corps, towards Le Beny Bocage, Vire and Condé, into some of the densest parts of the bocage. 7th Armoured, as part of XXX Corps, had now replaced 4 CLY with 5 DG, but was not needed in the opening stages of the operation. However, it was concentrated near an increasingly congested Caumont. Moving up later, it entered the fray on 2 August, being directed to move on Aunay; with 8 H, 1 RTR and 5 DG leading. Having encountered growing opposition on the high ground northwest of Sauques, more infantry — the Queen's Brigade — were brought up for a successful night attack, although the Germans immediately responded with counterattacks. One particularly fierce armoured counterattack even overran some elements of 5 RTR and the Norfolk Yeomanry. However, with 8 H reinforcing them it was eventually beaten off, with great loss to the enemy in both tanks and men.

It was at this point that the division underwent the changes in command that have already been mentioned above, Maj-Gen G L Verney, latterly the commander of 6 Guards

ONE DAY'S WORK

The speed of the advance through France and into the Low Countries is highlighted by one exploit of B Platoon of the Division's Petrol Company.

It was used on an ammunition lift in Holland and Belgium travelling Eindhoven-Louvain-Waterloo-Eindhoven-Nijmegen.

At Louvain the company collected 25pdr rounds, and at Waterloo the drivers had to dig out of a wood a large number of shells — they had been hidden there since 1940 and all of them had to be carried 40 yards to the vehicles. Each driver loaded 4.5 tons of shells like this and then had himself to unload them at Nijmegen.

On this trip the platoon covered 240 miles in 19 hours over roads that were crowded with transports and in many places almost ruined by pot-holes and collapsed verges.

THE TOWN COUNCIL
and THE CITIZENS
of GHENT

express their real veneration and gratitude to the gallant

Officers and Men of the 7ᵗʰ Armoured Division

who, on the 6ᵗʰ September 1944, delivered our City
from the bold and odious German enemy.
Glorify the heroic war-acts of the 7ᵗʰ Armoured
Division on the African and the European continent.
Bow deeply for the sacrifices brought by the 7ᵗʰ Armoured
Division for the liberty of our City and our Country.
Salute in the 7ᵗʰ Armoured Division the spirit of freedom
and opposition against all kind of tyranny of the English
people, who, alone resisted, in 1940, the strongest enemy
and so made possible the final victory.

Long live the 7ᵗʰ Armoured Division !

Ghent, the 6ᵗʰ September 1945.

Burgomaster :
Town Council :

Town Secretary :

Above and Right: The liberation of Ghent. An
illuminated address presented to 7th Armd Div by the
town council and citizens of Ghent soon after their
liberation on 6 September 1944, and a reciprocal
plaque from the division to the town made by the
division workshops.

Armd Bde, becoming GOC, whilst over 100 other long-serving officers and men were posted to other commands.

With fierce and continuous opposition being met in the centre of the division's advance, Gen Verney ordered a left-flanking movement by 22nd Armd Bde and 1/5th Queen's. This began on 4 September and by the 5th had reached Bonnemaison, then the high ground north of Hamars. Here it began to get bogged down because of difficulties navigating through an area of massive destruction caused by bombing, plus the considerable damage left after the ferocious fighting around Villers Bocage and Aunay, as well as enemy minefields and accurate defensive artillery fire. Nevertheless, the advance continued early on the 6th, edging north of Aunay, so as to make use of the still-intact road to La Vallée, which, although mined and defended, was cleared by nightfall. An artillery duel now ensued across the valley behind the village with the enemy on the slopes of Mt Pincon, whilst elsewhere the limitations of the terrain and the ferocity of the defence completely held up further progress. It was decided to mount another night assault to break the deadlock, which became a highly successful "textbook" operation featuring perfect "box-barrage" cooperation between the divisional infantry and artillery.

On 7 August the Germans in the west launched an unsuccessful counterattack against the Americans, in an attempt to contain them within the Cherbourg peninsula, which was destroyed primarily by Allied air power. The Americans then wheeled round to their left, with the aim of linking up with British and Canadians, so as to cut off some 50,000 enemy troops and much of his armour in the Falaise Pocket, and thus preventing further German attempts to contain the Allies in Normandy. As part of this operation, the division moved towards Condé in two columns, one (1 RTR and 1/7th Queens) along the Aunay-Condé road and the other (5 RTR, 5 DG,1/5th and 1/6th Queens) from the direction of the recent breakthrough at La Vallée. This, its last battle in the bocage, would be a terrible one, because the terrain virtually precluded the use of armour and had therefore to be fought mainly by the infantry — who bore the brunt of the casualties, including CO 1/5th Queen's, Lt-Col J B Ashworth, as well as many other officers and men. In fact, because of the persistent drain on manpower and equipment over this period of high attrition, the division soon no longer had the resources to operate at such a pace — it needed a rest, resupply and a refit for its tanks. It was consequently taken out of the line on 10 August, except for 11 H, 3 and 6 RHA and 5 DG, who remained with XXX Corps.

However, the fighting continued, so rest was not for long — the division being summoned back to action on 17 August, when it was able to escape from the constricting bocage into considerably easier terrain which was more open going, where the armour could often, but not always, lead.

The "Desert Rats" then advanced east from Caen towards the River Seine but were held up by having to navigate over the Dives, Vie, Touques, Orbec and Risle rivers, with almost all their bridges blown and determined enemy rearguards making good use of them all. On 17 August, the division was directed to advance on Livarot and then Lisieux, the Queen's Brigade leading with 8 H and 11 H fanned out across a wide front, searching to find any bridges still standing or other potential crossing places over the River Vie, whilst the armoured brigade brought up the rear. After initially making good progress they were met with stiff resistance and over the next 48 hours the battle raged, with substantial casualties to both sides. On 19 August an old forgotten bridge was found intact by 11 H the Vie was crossed and a bridgehead established towards Livarot. When the enemy realised what had happened he blew the main bridge into the town, cutting off some o his own forces. Nevertheless, the stubborn defence was eventually annihilated and the town taken. By the 21st the Engineers had re-bridged the Vie, brought across 22nd Armoured Bde and the division was now strung out along ten miles of road, fighting in three different places. At times its forward elements were cut off by enemy counterattacks, for the area around Lisieux was sufficiently well defended to prevent the bridgehead being further expanded.

Gen Verney now sought to find a way around the right flank, sending 1/7th Queen's and a squadron of 11 H across. However, resistance was too stiff and the going no good for armour. Finally, through dogged persistence, the enemy was worn down and wiped out. By mid-afternoon on 22 August, 1 RTR and 1/6th Queen's had penetrated well into the town — although it did not fall until the next day, under the combined weight of attacks from 51st Div from the south and 7th Armoured from the west.

The following day, despite counterattacks which were beaten back, the town was taken and the Orbec bridged. The advance then moved on to the next main German defensive line, based on the River Risle. As the division approached it was found that, although the road on either side of the bridge had been badly damaged by the RAF, Pont Authou was still standing, with the enemy established there in force. Further downstream the bridge at Montfort had been destroyed, but a forgotten and dilapidated old bridge was eventually found a mile beyond it. 5 DG then crossed over, attacked and took Pont Authou, which was then used as the main divisional route forward. Over the next three days, the division fought a series of piecemeal clearing actions against troops of varying quality, scattered over a wide area up to the River Seine, some of whom were tired and ready to surrender, while others were fresh, fanatical and well equipped. But the Battle of Normandy was drawing to a close, and on 28 August the division was pulled back for a quick rest and refit before the next stage of the long campaign, getting steadily nearer and nearer to the heart of the matter… Germany!

THE ADVANCE TO GHENT

7th Armoured was next to advance on Ghent as part of XII Corps under Lt-Gen Ritchie (a previous commander of Eighth Army in the desert). The Canadians were assigned to move along the coast on the left, with 11th Armoured Division on the right heading for Antwerp. The new British and Canadian tasks were firstly to move north and east, destroying "V-weapon" launching sites that were terrorising London; secondly, to take the major ports — in particular Antwerp — in order to shorten the Allied lines of supply. Having concentrated at Le Neuberg, and with 4th Armoured Brigade, the Royals and 10th Medium Regt, RA, all temporarily attached, the division's first task was to secure a bridgehead over

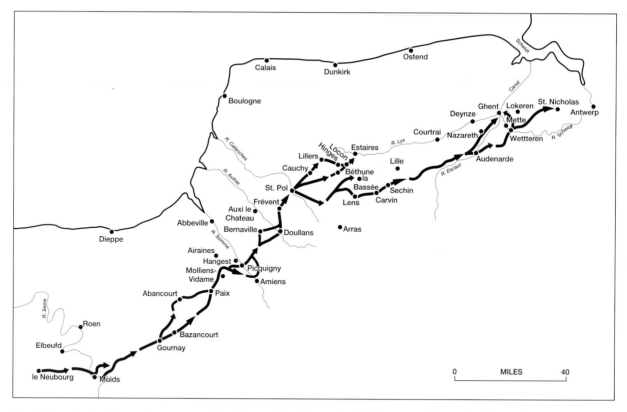

Above: Belgium & Holland, 6 September –
30 November 1944

Above right: Here is one of the dreaded PzKpfw VI
Tiger tanks, with its massive 88mm gun and thick
armour. Also on the photo (see 'X') is a *Panzerfaust*
anti-tank weapon, the larger versions being able to
penetrate 200mm of armour.

Right: Winter operations. 1 RTR and 2nd Devons took
Echt and Hingen on 18 January 1945. Here
infantrymen move carefully through the village at the
beginning of the assault.

the Somme. Crossing north of Amiens on 1 September in pouring rain, with much
congestion and coming up against a determined enemy rearguard, meant progress was
tortuously slow. Because of these problems other routes were looked for and another
bridge was found just out of the division's area of operations. With permission given to
use it, the Engineers were also ordered to bridge the river on the site of the destroyed
bridge at Picquigny. The Queen's Brigade, together with 5 RTR, now crossed over behind
4th Armd Bde and pushed on through the night to take the high ground near Bernaville,
capturing a flying-bomb site en route. There was now a dangerous threat on the left flank
from the German divisions in the Pas de Calais area, so the divisional attacks became a
series of hooks into this defence line. The countryside was also better suited for armour
and the speed of progress increased, although the river valleys ultimately focused on a
few crossing places. The 8 H and 1/5th Queen's crossed the Authie northwest of Doullens,
cleared Frévent and moved on to St Pol. However, at St Pol and at Auxi there was a strong
German presence and when it was realised progress was easier further west, the
emphasis of the advance changed accordingly.

By 4 September the division was now heading for the complicated canal and
coalmining area just north of Lille, where the defence was well entrenched and there was
especially fierce resistance. Fortunately, in order to get to Ghent on schedule, the division
was given permission to circumvent this dangerous area to the south and it was left to 1
RTR, with help from some elements of 5 DG, 1 RB and the Maquis, to break down and
overcome this stubborn defence.

Meanwhile, back at St Pol, on 3 September 11 H had fanned out on a three-squadron
front, and found an intact bridge over the La Bassée Canal, which it crossed, and then
assaulted the well-defended town of la Bassée. Then, while the rest of the division
remained in the difficult Béthune/Lille area, keeping the centre line open, a mixed group
of units from both brigades led by 11 H, made a dash for Ghent. They reached it the

Above: Members of the tank troop that provided protection for Tac HQ 7th Armd Div, seen here in Holland during the winter 1944-5. All wear the zippered tank oversuit which kept crewmen warm and dry inside their tanks.

following day after securing Oudenarde and entered the city to a rapturous welcome from the inhabitants. The Germans slowly withdrew north and remained in control of the north bank of the Scheldt.

The division stayed around Ghent, securing the city, mopping up pockets of resistance and bridging the Scheldt at Wettern, whilst slowly bringing up the elements left at Béthune and liaising with the invaluable Belgian resistance. The battered German Fifteenth Army was still in the area with some 11 divisions still dangerous. Because it was trying to escape eastwards, fighting its way home through the division's area of operations, Gen Verney ordered the destruction of all bridges over the River Lys and preparation for the same on the River Escaut. However, in the end the Germans retired northwards across the Scheldt estuary.

At the close of this phase the division had covered 220 miles in a week, taken over 1,000 prisoners and lost far fewer men than in the bocage battles (less than 100 as compared with 1,300). However, the supply lines were now awesomely long and as a result the division was very stretched out. Once again it had fought itself almost to a standstill, expending its resources to achieve its objectives. Its armoured brigade was down to about two thirds of its tanks and its infantry strength had been reduced by half.

Above: Getting ammunition ready for this BL 5.5in gun/howitzer, which is supporting armoured operations in Holland. It had a maximum range of 16,200yd and the shell weight was 100lb.

OPERATION MARKET GARDEN

The division was next moved to Malines for a brief spell, guarding the canal line between Herenthals and Antwerp, while other divisions (11th Armd and Guards Armd) forced strongly contested bridgeheads over the Albert and Escaut canals. Then on 17 September 1944 Operation Market Garden began. This operation was a daring gamble to foreshorten the war by means of a series of paratroop landings to capture vital bridges en route to Germany, being followed up by an armoured assault to link them all together. This was the reason for the "bridge too far" airborne landing at Arnhem. Unexpectedly strong enemy resistance, heavy casualties and bad weather all combined against the airborne troops, whilst the relieving ground forces failed to reach them. On 25 September, the battered survivors were pulled out. While the attempt to capture a bridge over the Lower Rhine had failed, the Allies still retained a valuable salient from which they would launch further assaults during the battle for Germany the following February. For the operation, XII Corps (of which the division was still a part) was moved into Holland with the task of guarding the western side of the attack corridor, while VIII Corps, with 11th Armoured Div, protected the eastern side. The terrain was very unsuitable for armour, with flat marshy "polder" and many dykes, as well as roads which

were both of poor quality and dangerously exposed to enemy fire. XII Corps was accordingly swung round westwards into Brabant to clear the northern shore and 7th Armoured instructed to push on to the River Maas. From 22 to 31 October, in a bitter, relentless attack, the division (Queen's Bde complete, 1 RTR, 8 H, 11 H and 1 RB), supported by minesweeping and flamethrowing tanks, slowly and deliberately eliminated the various strongpoints in that area and achieved its objectives, taking s'Hertogenbosch, Middelrode, Loop-on-Zond, Dongen and Oosterhout, then finally reaching the Maas.

Following these battles the division remained beside the Maas and was rested for 10 days. On 10 November it was moved to the eastern edge of the Second Army sector, taking over the line along the Maas and the Wessem Canal. The division then played a small part in the XII Corps offensive east of Wert, its task being to seize the lock gates at Panheel before the Germans destroyed them and flooded the area. In a ferocious battle with high casualties, involving 1/7th Queens and 8H, the lock gates were taken. The division was not involved in stopping the German Ardennes offensive of mid-December 1944, but instead remained on the Maas in freezing weather while it was rested, re-equipped and reorganised, and had its manpower brought back up to strength. The Queen's Brigade had suffered heavily in the previous months' fighting and the battalions

Above: HQ 22nd Armd Bde at Syke, on the southern approaches to Bremen in early April 1945. Note the temporary command post that has been set up, partly on one of the Cromwells, with two LOs/staff officers sitting outside the tank on chairs, numerous large aerials on the tank and behind it, and what looks like a skywave aerial on the roof of the nearby thatched cottage. *IWM — BU3348*

Left: A well-laden 7th Armd Div Cromwell passing through the ruined village of Borken, 30 March 1945. *IWM — BU 2895*

Left: Two members of 5 RTR looking at a knocked-out enemy anti-tank gun (a 7.5cm Pak 40 L/46) in Rethem on the Aller which they reached in early April 1945.

Above: Div HQ staff sorting through just some of the enormous numbers of maps that were needed to keep up with the rapid advance through Germany. One can imagine how difficult it was just folding a map in the confines of a tank turret — hence the need for some space to examine them properly. *IWM — BU3185*

Right: VE Day. D Sqn 11 H built this huge bonfire to celebrate "Victory in Europe", on 8 May 1945.

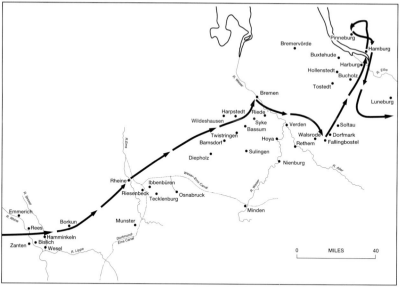

Above: Taking the war into the Reich. From the entry into Germany to end of the war, January 1945 – May 1945.

were therefore amalgamated, leaving only 1/5th Queen's in 131 Brigade, the other two battalions being replaced by 2nd Devons and 9th Durham Light Infantry, both from 50th Infantry Division. Maj-Gen L O Lyne, also from the Northumbrian Division, relieved Gen Verney and took over as GOC, whilst Verney went to Italy to command 6th Armoured Division.

ADVANCE INTO GERMANY

Designed to clear the area up to the River Roer, an operation (Blackcock) was conducted under the aegis of XII Corps and as a result 7th Armd had additional armour and troops temporarily attached — 8th Armd Bde and 155 Inf Bde from 52nd Infantry Division and later 1st Commando Bde.

The continuation of the freezing weather was essential to the operation's success, for a thaw and its muddy consequences would quickly bring an armoured division on the move to an abrupt halt.

On 13 January 1945 1/5th Queen's began the first preliminary attack, aided by flail tanks and an artillery barrage. The main assault went in on the 17th, with 9 DLI capturing Dieteren, the Queen's then leapfrogging forward to attack the next village — Susteren. An enemy counterattack was swiftly broken up by 3 RHA, with 1 RTR coming up in support, but the battle for Susteren was to be a costly affair in both armour and men and the next few days were a hard-fought and expensive struggle, winkling out defenders and forcing them to retreat or be killed. A partial thaw threatened to stymie the whole operation but the weather turned cold again and the ground refroze. On 18 January the Devons and 1 RTR captured Echt and the advance was continued northeastwards. On the 20th and 21st another fierce action was fought with high casualties by elements of 1 RB, 8 H and 9 DLI for possession of St Joost. On 22 January 5 DG and C Coy 1 RB moved on Montfort and later 1/5th Queen's with 5 RTR came up in support and the village was taken, along with many prisoners. On the 24th the division advanced along three axes, 1/5th Queens and 1 RTR to the east, aiming for Posterholt; the Devons and 5 DG in the centre, advancing northeast to the Roer; and 8 H with 1st Commando Bde in the west moving towards Linne. With the taking of all these objectives, Operation Blackcock was successfully concluded. The division was then rested until early February, holding the area it had taken whilst training for the next major operation — the crossing of the Rhine.

OPERATION PLUNDER

The plan was for Second Army to cross the Rhine at three points — at Rees with XXX Corps, and at Zanten and Wesel with XII Corps, of which 7th Armd was still a part. The specific divisional objective was Hamburg, approximately 200 miles away. By 26 March the river line had been taken and bridged and on the 27th 7th Armd Div, led by the ubiquitous 11 H, was the first British armoured division across. During the following week, it advanced to the Ems with the armoured brigade leading. Progress now slowed considerably, as each village and town had been so badly bombed they were often just rubble, and often, also, tenaciously defended. The Engineers were kept fully busy building fresh bridges and repairing roads, while the division now fought innumerable small-scale actions against ramshackle groups of the rapidly disintegrating German Army. On 1 April

Above left: End of the Third Reich. Men of 22nd Armd Bde display a pristine Nazi flag they have acquired. And by the look of the boxes on the back decks of their Cromwell, that isn't all they have liberated!

Below: Maj-Gen Lyne taking the salute at the dress rehearsal for the Victory Parade in Berlin

Above: Victory Parade, Berlin. Winston Churchill, accompanied by "Monty", Alanbrooke and Lyne, riding in an immaculate half-track, move slowly past Cromwells and their crews of the division. *IWM — BU9078*

Above right: Men of HQ 131 Bde and Signals Squadron marching towards the saluting base during the parade.

Right: OP tanks of 3 RHA move towards the saluting base.

the forward elements of the division, 5 DG and 9 DLI, broke into Rheine and the town was fully invested the following day. Meanwhile 11th Armd Div had crossed the Dortmund-Ems Canal on its way to Osnabrück, so 7th Armd now made use of this bridgehead to get 22nd Armd Bde across. 5 RTR also managed to seize a bridge over the Weser-Ems Canal and went on to take Diepholz, despite a rare attack by the Luftwaffe. 22nd Armd Bde was next tasked with the capture of Ibbenburen, but this proved to be a hard and costly nut to crack as it was ably defended by the diehard staff and trainees of a Wehrmacht officer training school, located in the town. Indeed it proved troublesome enough for the division to sidestep it and leave it to 53rd Infantry Div.

With the left flank now protected by a large marshy area and with 22nd Armd Bde leading, the division approached the next major obstacle of the River Weser. The bridge at Hoya was promptly blown on its arrival and the town was bristling with so many defenders and their artillery support that it was decided that the division would wheel north and attempt to cut off the German First Parachute Army rather than attempt to take the town or cross the river until sufficient forces had been concentrated there.

7 April saw 131 Brigade moving north towards Twistringen and then Bassum, which was heavily defended and did not fall until the following day under the combined weight of a converging two-pronged assault led by A Sqn 5 DG and A Coy 1 RB on the left and B Sqn 5 DG with a company of 9 DLI on the right. 155 Brigade then linked up with 131 Bde on 9 April at Bassum, having captured Barnstorf. Meanwhile, 22nd Armd Bde approached Bremen, 8 H and 1/5 Queen's taking Reide, while 11 H and 5 RTR captured Syke. By 10 April 9 DLI and 5 DG, plus a battery of Norfolk Yeomanry, had captured Harpstedt and Wildeshausen. All gains were held against counterattacks and consolidated. However, the battle for Bremen would be a more drawn-out affair and it was decided instead to send the division north to the Elbe and Harburg, to firstly cut the autobahn link with Hamburg, then assault that city itself. Once again the next 10 days were a bitter struggle against fanatical defenders pursuing a scorched earth policy of destroying everything, hiding and re-emerging behind the advance and making the most out of the heavily wooded and marshy terrain. They were also well equipped and supplied with all kinds of arms and plentiful ammunition from pre-prepared caches. However, the Allied war machine was now unstoppable and remorseless, and a surrounded and invaded Germany no longer had the resources to defend itself other than by these final desperate individual actions.

On 15 April 22nd Armd Bde crossed the Rethem bridgehead, by evening Walsrode had been occupied and the following day the brigade advanced in two columns on Soltau — one with 8 H along the main road and the other with 1 RTR across country further to the north. Opposition was stiff at Fallingbostel but it was comprehensively cleared by the

1939 1945

AFRICA
WESTERN DESERT
EL ALAMEIN TOBRUK BENGHAZI
TRIPOLI MARETH TUNIS

ITALY
SALERNO NAPLES VOLTURNO

FRANCE
NORMANDY THE SEINE ROUBAIX

BELGIUM
OUDENARDE GHENT MALINES

HOLLAND
EINDHOVEN TILBURG THE MAAS

GERMANY
THE RHINE AHAUS SOLINGEN
NIENBURG SOLTAU HAMBURG

BERLIN

Above: When 7th Armd Div entered Berlin in the summer of 1945, it erected a stone monument at the end of the autobahn. Later, roadworks in the area made it necessary to move the monument, so it was taken to the UK and set up in the grounds of the RMA Sandhurst, where it remains today.

Queen's and 8 H, who liberated nearby two large prisoner-of-war camps, one of which had already been taken over by the inmates and was being run with iron precision by a paratroop RSM.

On 17 April 22nd Armd Bde bypassed Soltau, leaving it to 5 DG and 7 RTR with their Crocodile flamethrower tanks, and moved across boggy ground towards Tostedt, which fell on the 18th. With Bucholz captured the next day by 131st Brigade, the First German Parachute Army had now been squeezed into a pocket between Bremen and Hamburg. The division again found itself somewhat spread out, with more than one task in hand. The prime aim was to still cut the autobahn between Bremen and Hamburg and capture Harburg; the secondary aim was to root out the last hardcore German forces hiding in the woods in the Soltau area.

The autobahn was cut at Hollenstadt on 19 April by 8 H and 1/5 Queen's, who then turned east and fought their way inch by inch into the Elbe valley. These final actions took place to the south and west of Hamburg, and involved rounding up or destroying ragtag groups of Nazi fanatics including police, army, SS, Gestapo, paratroops, marines, submarine crews and even stevedores, most of whom were determined to die with the end of the Third Reich

SURRENDER OF HAMBURG

On 29 April 1945 a deputation was sent to the British lines from Hamburg to begin the surrender negotiations for the city and, under the threat of a renewed air assault, the city quickly surrendered. Thus, on 3 May units of the Division drove unopposed into the shattered city. Two days later, on 5 May, the hostilities ceased at 8am. The Division now became an army of occupation, remaining in the area it was located when the fighting stopped and beginning to process the huge numbers of German troops that were coming west to surrender.

BERLIN PARADE 1945 AND CHURCHILL'S ADDRESS

On 21 June 1945 at 10am the guns roared out over ruined Berlin — British guns fired by 3 RHA, to signify the start of the "End of the War Parade". The "Desert Rats" were given the signal honour of playing a major role in this parade, which was a fitting epilogue after they had fought their way from the deserts of North Africa, through Italy and Northwest Europe, from Mersa Matruh to the Baltic — "a march unsurpassed through all the story of war," as Prime Minister Winston Churchill put it. What thoughts must have passed through the minds of the veterans as they saluted their great war leader! FLOREAT JERBOA!

Above: From February to May 1942, 7th Armoured Brigade conducted a heroic withdrawal through Burma acting as rearguard for the withdrawing British and Commonwealth forces for most of the way. 7 Hussars and 2 RTR were equipped with the small M3 Light "Honey" tanks and had to fight all their way back to the Chindwin River.

Left: On reaching the Chindwin, they then had to destroy their tanks to prevent them being used by the Japanese, so the engines were drained of oil and run until they seized. Then the crews had to make a long and dangerous trek into India, moving by night and hiding up by day. However, they made it safely and went on to fight against the Germans and Italians in Italy.

INSIGNIA, CLOTHING & EQUIPMENT

Above: This insignia denotes a major in 44 RTR. The major's crown has the yellow backing of the RAC/cavalry and sits atop a yellow and red regimental flash of the 44th Royal Tank Regiment. At the top of the sleeve sits the Desert Rat, properly the jerboa, in black and white, signifying 4th Armoured Brigade. Below that is the red and yellow service stripe of the Royal Armoured Corps. Last but not least is the "arm badge, tank" worn on the right sleeve by all ranks of the Royal Tank Regiment.

FORMATION INSIGNIA

The Red Rat

7th Armoured's initial emblem was inherited from the Mobile Division, being a plain white circle on a scarlet ground. However, soon after Gen O'Moore Creagh took command, he decided that the circle should contain some symbol that was truly representative of the division's desert background. He chose the Greater Egyptian Jerboa (Jaculus Orientalis), a tough little rodent that lived in the Arabian desert. It was sand coloured, with a long balancing tail and massive back legs which enabled it to leap six feet from a standing start! The next problem was to find a live one to copy, but after much searching one was located in Cairo Zoo and the first "Desert Rat Rampant" was drawn on a sheet of hotel notepaper by Mrs Creagh and Mrs Peyton (wife of the GSO3). This was transferred in flaming scarlet to the white circle on the divisional commander's flag by Peter Hordern (then serving as a liaison officer at Div HQ) and thence onto every vehicle and every topee flash.

The Green Rat

At the end of 1941, 7th Armoured Brigade left the division and went to Burma. It kept its jerboa emblem, but changed its colour to green — presumably to blend in with the jungle.

The Black Rat

When 4th Armoured Brigade also left the division (after the capture of Tobruk) it also kept its rat but not only changed its colour to black, but also put its tail up over its head. Not to be outdone, the Queen's Brigade used a black jerboa in a red oval as its vehicle sign.

The Stag's Head

Certain other armoured brigades also had their own brigade sign on their vehicles. Within 7th Armoured Division this applied only to the 22nd Armd Bde, whose red stag's head on a white square is sometimes to be seen on the opposite mudguard, balancing the divisional sign.

A Shoulder Patch

When the division was resting in the Homs-Tripoli area in the summer of 1943, after the Axis surrender in North Africa, the first shoulder patch appeared — it was the original scarlet jerboa on a khaki square, but it was not worn universally because it was in short

supply. Then when the division left Italy, the GOC gave orders that shoulder patches for the whole division should be produced and be ready for issue when they reached the UK. However, the clothing firm selected by the War Office to make them had its own ideas on what a jerboa should look like and the result was more akin to a kangaroo than a jerboa (hence some rude remarks from Aussie troops!). The powers that be were adamant that they were to be used, so the altered flashes had to be accepted, although the original scarlet rat was still used as the vehicle sign.

Ever since then the red/brown "kangaroo-like" jerboa on its black background has remained the emblem of the division and then, after the disbandment of the division, that of the 7th Armoured Brigade, while 4th Armd Bde has retained the black rat. To quote Gen Verney: "Whatever his shape, his colour or his attitude, the Jerboa remains the farthest travelled animal with the longest fighting record. Long may he be honoured. *FLOREAT JERBOA!*"

Vehicle Signs in the Desert
In addition to the divisional signs, there were other ways of recognising vehicles belonging to the division, for example:

a. Overall colour. In the early days of the war (1939-41), the standard camouflage painting for British AFVs was in straight-edged patterns of either black with green, or silver-grey with slate-grey, on top of a basic light stone colour. There might well also be the white/red/white or white/black/white British identification stripes painted on the side of the turret or body of the tank (perhaps on the side plates).

Above left: The original topee flash, which became the vehicle sign for the newly formed 7th Armoured Division, first drawn by Mrs Peyton, then in flaming scarlet by Lt (now Col Retd) Peter Hordern, who was at the time one of the LOs in HQ 7th Armd Div.

Above: Final divisional jerboa shoulder patch. This sign was introduced when the division reached the UK in December 1943 and was worn throughout the rest of the war and on until disbandment. It is now worn by 7th Armd Bde.

b. Unit Identification. Units were identified by two numerals in white on a red, green, or green and white square, for example:

Div HQ:		a red square containing the divisional sign above a white "99" on a black square
Armd Car Regt:	11H	black "14" on a square (top half green, bottom half white)
7th Armd Bde:	1RTR	white "24" on a red square
	8H	white "25" on a red square
	3H	white "26" on a red square
4th Armd Bde:	7H	white "28" on a green square
	2RTR	white "29" on a green square
	6RTR	white "30" on a green square

Above: A group of fitters, belonging to A Squadron, 5 RTR, pose on top of one of their vehicles, a heavy utility 4 x 2 Canadian Ford C11ADF that was widely used in North Africa, often with the complete top removed. Note both the divisional sign and the "A" Sqn triangle (also the mixture of dress/undress — typical fitters!).

Above right: A excellent shot of an "acquired" Mercedes-Benz 170VK staff car. Note that as well as the "Desert Rat" sign, there is also the 22nd Armd Bde Stag's Head on the opposite mudguard, plus "53" which signifies that it belongs to the junior armoured regiment in the brigade, namely 5 RTR.

Right: War Imminent! NCOs of 1 RTR wearing the two-piece black denims, plus in most cases solar topees, as they are briefed on 24 August 1939. Note also the black hose-tops, worn by the SSM in KD, goggles (on the sergeant with the beret) and the slung respirators which some are carrying.

Vehicle Signs in Northwest Europe

By the time the division landed in Northwest Europe, the standard vehicle colour was olive drab and camouflaged patterns had largely been discontinued (however, during the winter of 1944/5, many AFVs were painted with whitewash to help them blend in with the snowy scenery). Unit identification numbers were still being used, but had changed (see table below), as had the colour of the background squares, both of which had now been standardised within the British Army as a whole.

Examples of Standard Vehicle Markings as used in NW Europe

Unit	Number	Arm or Service Colour of Background
HQ Armd Div (incl FSS and Int Sect)	40	Black
Armd Recce Regt	43	Green/blue horizontal
Armd Car Regt (Corps Tps)	44	Green/blue horizontal
Field Regts RA	64, 65	Red/blue horizontal
Atk Regt	77	Red/blue horizontal
LAA Regt	73	Red/blue horizontal
Field Sqns RE	41, 46	Blue
Fd Pk Sqn	42	Blue
HQ Armd Bde	50	Red
3 x armd regt	51, 52, 53	Red
Mot Bn	54	Red
HQ Inf Bde	60	Green
3 x inf bns	61, 62, 63	Green
Armd Bde Coy RASC	81	Red/green diagonal
Inf Bde Coy RASC	83	Red/green diagonal
Div Tps Coy RASC	84	Red/green diagonal
Fd Amb	90	Black
Lt Fd Amb	89	Black
FDS	93	Black
Fd Hygiene Sect	92	Black
Ord Fd Pk	97	Blue/red/blue
Armd Bde Wksp	99	Blue/yellow/red horizontal
Inf Bde Wksp	100	Blue/yellow/red
Pro Coy	43	Black
Postal Unit	44	Black
Sigs	*	Blue/white horizontal

* carry number of formation/unit to which they are attached

Other Vehicle Signs
Squadron signs as used throughout the war by all formations were the normal diamond (HQ), triangle (A Sqn), square (B Sqn) and circle (C Sqn), sometimes with troop numbers inside. Initially, in the desert, the senior regiment in the brigade had its signs in red, the second senior yellow and the junior regiment blue. Colour was, however, often dispensed with and they appeared in white or black.

Tank Names
These normally followed a standard pattern as laid down within regimental standing orders, although on occasions crews might choose their own names. For example, RTR regiments used names beginning with the appropriate letter of the alphabet for the regiment, eg in 1 RTR all tank names began with "A", in 2 RTR with a "B" and so on. However, there were many variations and especially at times of stress new tanks were often unnamed.

Opposite: The distinctive black beret and silver cap badge of the RTC/RTR. The cap badge with its scroll reading 'Fear Naught' dates from 18 October 1923. The beret was copied from the WWI headgear worn by French chasseurs alpins. The entire Royal Armoured Corps took to wearing black berets with individual regimental badges in 1940. Note also the service respirator worn in the ready position on the chest.

Left: RAC crash helmet, 1939 issue. Made from a number of panels it sported ventilation holes with rubber grommets. The helmet gave no protection from bullets or shrapnel, only bumps from the tank.

Below left: Hard fibre RAC crash helmet, 1941. This gave increased protection with a padded front section.

Below: Side view of the hard fibre RAC crash helmet with an additional side flap for wireless operators. This one has earphones wired for the WS19, 15 watt AFV wireless.

Right: The crew of this A13 cruiser tank belonging to 2 RTR have just fought the Battle of Beda Fomm, so are relaxing. Note the leather jerkins worn by the commander sitting by the bivvie and his gunner (with beard). They knocked out 20 Italian tanks that day! The gunner wears his pistol in a low-slung holster, with the strap around his upper leg. All wear denims and RTR berets.

UNIFORMS, PERSONAL EQUIPMENT AND PERSONAL ARMS

Uniforms

When war was declared the introduction of the new battledress (BD) and the new range of webbing equipment was still in progress. This uniform was, of course, primarily designed for wear in temperate climates, so during the division's initial years in North Africa and Italy, khaki drill uniform was worn — which comprised lightweight sand-coloured khaki tunics or shirts, long/short trousers worn with boots or shoes, long stockings and hose-tops (with shorts). This is not to say that BD was never worn in the Middle East — it was certainly most welcome during the bitterly cold desert nights or in the mountains of Tunisia and Italy, where even greatcoats and cap comforters were often worn. In addition, the officers in particular added various items of unofficial dress — suede desert boots with crepe rubber soles, coloured silk scarves, sheepskin coats and the like. Indeed, such items became synonymous with the "Desert Rats", thanks to the unforgettable "Two Types" cartoons by Jon and the example set by their C-in-C, "Monty"! Once they returned to Northwest Europe, BD became the order of the day, although coloured scarves still could be seen. The colder the weather became, the more essential became winter clothing. AFV crewmen were fortunate to have a special zipped oversuit to keep them warm and dry, whilst the stout brown leather sleeveless jerkin which had its beginnings in the Great War was much sought after. Prewar headgear, such as the solar topee, lasted for a few months in the Western Desert, but was soon replaced, either by the regular pattern steel helmet, or individual unit headgear — berets, for example, being much more convenient to wear inside a tank. In short, the soldiers of the division wore most of the normal types of British Army uniforms appropriate to the theatre of operations, their individuality being maintained by their "Desert Rat" flashes, their unit headgear and cap badges, and for some, their unofficial items of dress.

VEHICLES, WEAPONS AND EQUIPMENT

The same general rule applied to personal weapons. Pistols, rifles, light machine guns, grenades etc were all standard British Army issue, although of course, in some cases, American weapons and equipment were used — eg the Browning machine gun (.30 and .50 calibre) and the Thompson sub-machine gun.

Below: An excellent photograph of HQ Support Group staff, 7th Armd Div, in the desert in 1940. In the centre of the rear row with his hands on chest is Brig "Strafer" Gott. Most wear KD shorts and shirts, some wear suede desert boots, RTR berets, forage caps and one an issue pullover (see his solar topee on the table behind the group). I would give them nought out of 10 for their camouflage on their Command Vehicle!

Tanks

Main Types of Tanks Used by 7th Armoured Division

Yrs of main use	Type	Name/Nomenclature	Weight (tons)	Crew	Armament
1939-40	Medium	Vickers Mark III	13.5	5	1 x 3pdr, 3 x MG
1939-41	Light	Vickers Mark VI	5.5	3	1 x hy MG, 1 x MG
1939-41	Cruiser	Mark I (A9)	12	6	1 x 2pdr, 3 x MG
1939-42	Cruiser	Mark II (A10)	13.75	4	1 x 2pdr, 1 x MG
1939-42	Cruiser	Mark III (A13)	14.75	4	1 x 2pdr, 1 x MG
1941-3	Cruiser	Mark VI (A15)	19	5	1 x 2pdr, 2 x MG
(The Crusader III was 0.75-ton heavier, mounted a 6pdr gun and had two less crewmen)					
1941-5	Light (US)	Stuart I ("Honey")	12.5	4	1 x 37mm, 2 x MG
1942-4	Medium (US)	M3 (Grant I)	28.5	6	1 x 75mm, 1 x 37mm, 1 x MG
1942-5	Medium (US)	M4 (Sherman)	30	5	1 x 75mm, 2 x MG
1944-5	Medium (US/UK)	Sherman VC (Firefly)	32	4	1 x 17pdr, 1 x MG
(This was the British upgunned Sherman and was issued on a scale of one per tank troop)					
1944/45	Cruiser	A27M (Cromwell)	19	5	1 x 6pdr, 2 x MG
1945	Cruiser	A34 (Comet)	35.2	5	1 x 77mm, 2 x MG

Examples of Other Types of AFVs Used

Type	Name/Nomenclature	Weight (tons)	Crew	Armament
Scout Car	Daimler Dingo	2.8-3.15	2	1 x LMG
Scout Car	Humber	3.39	3	1 x LMG
Armoured car	Rolls (1924 pattern)	3.8	4	1 x MG
Armoured car	Morris CS9/LAC	4.2	4	1 x MG, 1 x Boys
Armoured car	Humber	6.85	3	1 x hy MG, 1 x MG (MkIV had 1 x 37mm gun)
Armoured car	Daimler	6.8	3	1 x 2pdr, 1 x MG
Carrier	Bren No 2	3.75	3	1 x LMG or 1 x atk rifle
Carrier	Scout	3.3	3-4	1 x LMG or 1 x atk rifle

Opposite: Tank crew overalls were introduced in 1942. Made of unlined heavy cotton they had a water repellant finish and adjustable wrist and ankle buttoned tabs. A zipped vent on both sides above the hip gave access to clothing underneath, above each is an open top pocket closed with a press stud. On the right hip is an additional dressing pocket. On the left thigh is a map pocket and on the upper right thigh a shaped flap for a revolver.

Left: This group of four infantrymen all wear KD shirt and shorts, together with boots, webbing gaiters and long stockings, plus webbing belts, ammunition pouches, service respirators and steel helmets. All are armed with the Rifle No 1 MkIII, SMLE (Short Magazine Lee Enfield) rifle as used in World War I. One of the finest rifles ever produced, it could be fitted with a long, 18in, bayonet.

Below left: Two members of a Sherman tank crew lift down the tank's coaxially mounted .30-cal M1919 Browning machine gun for cleaning. The M1919 had an air-cooled barrel, a rate of fire of 400-500rpm and was fed by a 250-round belt.

Below: Tank crewman holding a brew and a 9in cruciform bayonet as fitted to the SMLE's successor, the Rifle No 4 MkI. He is armed with the usual tank crewman's .38in six-shot Pistol, Revolver, No 2 MkI which was taken into service in 1932.

"B" Vehicles
Whilst the division used the standard range of British wheeled vehicles as can be found in any similar British formation serving in the same theatre, the early command vehicles (CVs) as used in the Western Desert deserve special mention. The bodies of the orginal CVs were made of 5-ply wood with a zinc covering. When they were sent back to Cairo to be armoured, the wood was removed, angle iron clamped on to the chassis and South African boiler plate then bolted on using thousands of 3/16in bolts. Consequently, there were myriad bolt ends sticking through the armour — a most uncomfortable arrangement for those inside!

ARTILLERY

During the wartime years the division used the full gamut of British Army artillery as far as field, anti-tank and light anti-aircraft weapons were concerned. The table below lists the main types in each category.

Anti-tank

Description	Max Effective Range	Rate of Fire	Comments
Ordnance QF 2pdr	600yd	20-22rpm	heavy gun, so had to be towed or carried "portee"
Ordnance QF 6pdr	5,500yd	10rpm	by 1943 it could not penetrate the frontal armour of heavy enemy tanks
Ordnance QF 17pdr	10,000yd	10rpm	very effective, could penetrate 130mm of armour at 1,000yd

Anti-aircraft

Description	Effective Ceiling	Rate of Fire	Comments
Bofors 40mm	5,000ft	120rpm	Highly effective, widely used. (Swedish-designed). By 1945, the British had three main Marks, six specialised and two lightweight mountings and five different firing platforms.

Field

Description	Max Range	Shell Weight	Comments
Ordnance QF 18pdr	11,100yd	18.5lb	In widespread service prewar
Ordnance QF 25pdr	12,000yd		
MkI and MkII	(MkII — 13,400yd)	25lb	Rugged and dependable. By 1944, most were MkII
(Both the 18 and 25pdrs were towed by a Field Artillery Tractor 4 x 4 — at first the Guy "Quad" Ant, then the Morris C8 "Quad".)			

Medium

Description	Max Range	Shell weight	Comments
QF 4.5in Howitzer	6,600yd	34.5lb	In service prewar, a few saw action in desert
BL 5.5in MkIII Gun	16,200yd	100lb	One of the best British field guns

Above left: 'That bint from the Sweet Melody promised she'd write!' Jon's jaunty 'Two Types' were famous for their eccentricities of dress — the suede boots, silk scarves, corduroy trousers, sheepskin coats and all the rest; however, such garments did have a serious, practical side as well. For example, the scarves gave the wearer protection against the choking clouds of dust that swiftly caked everything during a sandstorm, including eyes, nostrils and throat, whilst the sheepskin coats kept out the bitter cold of the desert nights far better than the average army issue greatcoat. And all these goods were temptingly on display in the shop windows in Cairo — with no need for clothing coupons either! Even when they left the desert sands for the rainstorms of Italy, the Desert Rats still kept wearing their trademark garments, as did Monty, who always had an eye for wearing comfortable, practical, slightly eccentric clothes, that were not always exactly the King's uniform.

Above: This RAOC fitter is hard at work, wearing BD and a battered, almost shapeless, SD cap. All Ordnance Corps fitters automatically became craftsmen in the Corps of Electrical & Mechanical Engineers when the new corps was formed in May 1942.

Left: This 6 RTR crew was photographed at Burg el Arab in October 1942. Note the mixture of KD and one-piece denims being worn. The crew stands in front of its American Grant M3 Medium tank, which had its 75mm main gun in a side sponson and only a 37mm in the turret.

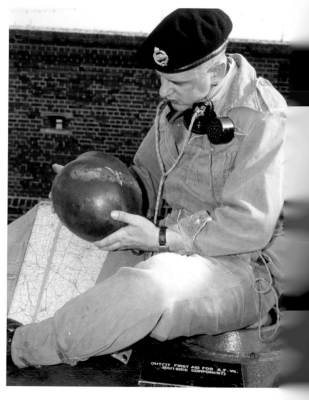

Left and Below: Tank crewman of the 1st King's Dragoon Guards wearing his camouflaged oversuit. Designed towards the end of the war for operating in temperate climates, it has two full length zips running down the front for quick dressing and easy access to wounds. The left chest pocket has pencil loops.

Opposite, Above left: The denim tank suit had integral braces which allowed the top half of the suit to be opened up and dropped to the waist while still being supported. The suit also had a rear hip pocket unique to the denim overalls.

Opposite, Above right: The "Pixie Suit" (properly Tank Crew Oversuit, 1943). Made of heavyweight cotton and fully lined with wool fabric, it had two throat-to-ankle zips and adjustable wrist and ankle tabs. It had two internal supporting braces and seven external patch pockets, two side pockets and three internal pockets.

Opposite, Below left: The RAC steel helmet gave better protection from shrapnel and bullets than previous headgear. The epaulettes are of strengthened cloth to supply a useful handhold when necessary.

Opposite, Below right: An RTR radio operator on top of a Sherman. In his pocket is a hand-held microphone and around his neck the headphones for his W519 wireless set. He is looking at a Fallschirmjäger helmet.

PEOPLE

Above: First and last. Field Marshal Viscount Montgomery talks to Gen Percy Hobart and Gen "Pip" Roberts, who were the actual first and last commanders of the 7th Armoured Division, although neither commanded the division during the war. When the photo was taken (in Berlin at the Victory Parade) Hobart was GOC 79th Armd Div and Roberts was GOC 11th Armd Div. *IWM — BU10669*

PERCY "HOBO" HOBART (1885–1976)

Major-General Sir Percy Cleghorn Stanley Hobart KBE, CB, DSO, MC — "Hobo" as he was known to all — was responsible for the initial training of the Mobile Division and thus the architect of much of its greatness. After being unfairly "retired" because he had fallen out with those in higher authority who knew nothing about tanks and armoured warfare, he was rescued from obscurity (a LCpl in the Home Guard!) by Winston Churchill and would later go on to form and train both 11th Armd Div and 79th Armd Div. As historian Sir Basil Liddell Hart said of him: "To have moulded the best two British armoured divisions of the war was an outstanding achievement, but Hobart made it a "hat trick" by his subsequent training of the specialised 79th Armoured Division, the decisive factor on D-Day."

"DICKIE" CREAGH (1892–1970)

Major-General Sir Michael O'Moore Creagh, KBE, MC led the division through its earliest triumphs against the Italians, including its first major battle at Sidi Barrani in 1940. His tenure of command was the longest during the war. It was he who took the bold decision to send a "Flying Column" (Combe Force) southwest across the virtually unmapped Libyan Desert to cut off the Italians at Sidi Saleh/Beda Fomm. This daring stroke led to the surrender of the *entire* Italian Tenth Army on 5-7 February 1941.

"STRAFER" GOTT (1897–1942)

Lieutenant-General W. H. E. "Strafer" Gott CB, DSO, MC began his career in the division as its first wartime GSO 1; later he commanded the Support Group. After commanding 7th Armd Div he went on to become commander XIII Corps and in August 1942 was appointed to command the Eighth Army. Tragically, whilst flying back to Cairo from the battle area a few days later, his aircraft was shot down by a German fighter. He survived the crash, but was killed by machine gun fire whilst rescuing others from the wreckage.

"JOCK" CAMPBELL (1894–1942)

Major-General J. C. Campbell VC, DSO, MC was perhaps the most famous of all "Desert Rats", his name being a byword for courage through the division. He was awarded the

Victoria Cross at Sidi Rezegh in November 1941, whilst commanding the Support Group. It was he who conceived the idea of forming mobile columns to harass the Italians — called "Jock Columns" after him. He was killed when his staff car overturned on a clay road near Halfaya Pass.

FRANK MESSERVY (1893–1974)

Lieutenant-General Sir Frank Walter Messervy CB, DSO took over the division after commanding 4th Indian Division. Known as the "Bearded Man" because he tended not to shave in battle. Knew little about tanks and was commanding when Div HQ was captured by the Germans, but managed to bluff them into believing he was a batman, escaped with other members of his staff and rejoined Div HQ the following day! He went on to command IV Corps in Burma.

"WINGY" RENTON (1898–1972)

Major-General James Malcolm Leslie Renton CB, DSO, OBE was known as "Wingy" Renton because he had lost an arm whilst commanding 2RB during the battle at Sidi Saleh in 1941, later commanded the Support Group, 7th Motor Bde, during the Gazala battles.

LORD HARDING (1896–1989)

Field Marshal, The Lord Harding of Petherton GCB, CBE, DSO, MC took over command after serving as Chief of Staff to Gen Sir Richard O'Connor and his successors in the early days in the desert. Fearless and brilliant, he was responsible for the division's breakout at El Alamein in October 1942. Badly wounded near Tarhuna on 20 January 1943, he recovered and continued a distinguished career, becoming C-in-C Far East (1949-51), C-in-C BAOR (1951-2), CIGS

Top: "Strafer" Gott being driven by "Jock" Campbell. Both men would command the division and be killed in accidents in the desert. *IWM — E7401*

Above: Frank Messervy—the "Bearded Man", as he was known—was captured and escaped during one fluid operation in the desert by pretending to be a private soldier. *IWM — E7506*

Right: The longest-serving member of HQ 7th Armd Div was Capt "Richie" Richardson BEM, who served continuously with Div HQ from August 1939 to January 1957, under no fewer than 16 GOCs! He is being congratulated by Gen Sir John Hackett. Note the board of GOCs behind them.

(1952-3), then Governor and C-in-C Cyprus (1955-7). Montgomery called him "that little tiger".

"BOBBIE" ERSKINE (1899–1965)

General Sir George W. E. J. Erskine GCB, KBE, DSO commanded during the memorable advance from Tripoli to Tunis and throughout the short campaign in Italy. He also launched the division into Northwest Europe. A man of great integrity and considerable physical and moral courage, he was commanding during the debacle at Villers Bocage in June 1944 and was "sacked" by Montgomery along with the corps commander, Gen Bucknall. Nevertheless, he went on to become C-in-C East Africa during the Mau Mau rebellion and, on retirement, Lt Governor and C-in-C Jersey.

GERALD VERNEY (1900–1957)

Major-General Gerald Lloyd Verney, DSO, MVO was personally appointed by "Monty" to

take command of the Desert Rats in Normandy on 4 August 1944, after the division's disappointing showing in the bocage. Verney commented, in the history of the division (which he wrote postwar), that before the battles of Caumont he had been warned to look out for the transport of the 7th Armoured on the road, because its march discipline was "non-existent!" He also said that they "greatly deserved the criticism they received". A no-nonsense Guardsman, Verney soon had them "firing on all cylinders" again. He left in November 1944 to command 6th Armoured Division.

"LEW" LYNE (1999–1970)

Major-General Lewis Owen Lyne CB, DSO took over command of the division on 22 November 1944, when Gen Verney went to Italy to command 6th Armoured Division. Gen Lyne had commanded 50th Northumbrian Division in

Top: Field Marshal The Lord Harding of Petherton, GCB, CBE, DSO, MC, late SLI. The "Little Tiger" as "Monty" called him, was a brilliant and fearless commander. *IWM — E9612*

Normandy, when Gen Graham was injured, until it became a training division in the UK. He would then command the "Desert Rats" on the final lap through the Siegfried Line, into Germany and on to the surrender of Hamburg and the end of the war. Postwar he was the first Military Governor of the British Zone of Berlin, then Director Staff Duties at the War Office, before retiring in 1949.

Above: Gen Sir George Erskine GCB, KBE, DSO, late KRRC. Bobbie Erskine commanded at the end in North Africa, all through Italy, back to the UK and on into France on D+1, making him the second longest-serving GOC. *IWM — NA7450*

"PIP" ROBERTS (1906–1997)

Major-General George Philip Bradley Roberts CB, DSO, MC was a charismatic wartime commander of 11th Armoured Division, and rated the best British armoured divisional commander of the war, Gen "Pip" Roberts was the first (and only) peacetime commander of 7th Armoured Division. He was no stranger to the division, having been the DAQMG when the Italians invaded Egypt in 1940, GSO2 during the Brevity and Battleaxe operations, CO of 3 RTR, commander 22nd Armoured Brigade and had

commanded the division for four days (20–24 January 1943) when Gen Harding was wounded. He would command the "Desert Rats" through the early postwar days to their first disbandment in March 1948. He then became Director of the Royal Armoured Corps and retired from the Army in September 1949. His book *From the Desert to the Baltic* is a very readable account of all his wartime battles.

Above left: Maj-Gen G. L. Verney DSO, MVO, late Brigade of Guards, who took over the "Desert Rats" from Erskine soon after the Villers Bocage debacle, seen here with "Monty", his "Desert Rat" very visible. *IWM — B 10387*

"MONTY" (1887–1976)

Above: Maj-Gen L. O. Lyne CB, DSO, last wartime commander of the division, took the division into Germany and all the way to Berlin. Here he tries out a bridge built by divisional Sappers at Nienburg over the River Weser on 13 April 1945. *IWM — BU 3440*

In addition to those already mentioned above, there were a number of senior officers — corps and army commanders mainly — whose actions had a direct bearing on the fortunes of the division. I have tried to mention these VIPs in the main body of the text. However, there is one who must be mentioned here as his influence on the "Desert Rat" was greater than that of anyone else. This was of course "Monty" — Field Marshal Bernard Law Montgomery, 1st Viscount of Alamein — who was probably Britain's most well known and charismatic senior commander of World War II. He was also one of the longest-serving and most successful Allied field commanders, coming into prominence when he took over the Eighth Army in North Africa and subsequently winning the battles of Alam Halfa and El Alamein. His further success in North Africa, Sicily and Italy made him the obvious choice to command 21st Army Group in Northwest Europe and he deliberately selected 7th Armoured Division to add battle experience to the largely untested Allied forces that would follow-up the initial landings in Normandy, bringing it back from Italy for that specific purpose. Therefore, he was understandably annoyed by its initial disappointing showing in the difficult bocage country in Normandy. He took drastic action to solve this problem by changing the corps, divisional and brigade commanders, whom he considered were responsible. He continued to command 21st Army Group throughout the battle in Europe. Postwar he was CIGS and deputy supreme commander of NATO Forces.

GENERAL OFFICERS COMMANDING 7th ARMD DIVISION

From	Status	Name
03.09.1939	GOC	Maj-Gen P. C. S. Hobart
16.11.1939	acting GOC	Brig J. A. L. Caunter
04.12.1939	GOC	Maj-Gen. M. O'M. Creagh
01.04.1941	acting GOC	Brig J. A. L. Caunter
13.04.1941	GOC	Maj-Gen. Sir M. O'M. Creagh
03.09.1941	GOC	Maj-Gen W. H. E. Gott
06.02.1942	GOC	Maj-Gen J. C. Campbell
23.02.1942	acting GOC	Brig A. H. Gatehouse
09.03.1942	GOC	Maj-Gen F. W. Messervy
19.06.1942	GOC	Maj-Gen. J. M. L. Renton
14.09.1942	GOC	Maj-Gen A. F. Harding
20.01.1943	acting GOC	Brig G. P. B. Roberts
24.01.1943	GOC	Maj-Gen G. W. E. J. Erskine
04.08.1944	GOC	Maj-Gen G. L. Verney
22.11.1944	GOC	Maj-Gen L. O. Lyne

VICTORIA CROSS WINNERS

During World War II members of the 7th Armoured Division won three Victoria Crosses. All three were awarded for conspicuous bravery during the battle of Sidi Rezegh on 21 November 1941. Here are details of their citations:

Above: Brigadier (Acting) John Charles Campbell DSO MC, Royal Horse Artillery.

Above right: 2nd Lieutenant George Ward Gunn MC, Royal Horse Artillery.

Right: Rifleman John Beeley, 1st Battalion The King's Royal Rifle Corps.

"JOCK" CAMPBELL (1894–1942)

Brigadier (Acting) John Charles Campbell DSO, MC of the Royal Horse Artillery's citation reads:

"On November 21st 1941, Brigadier Campbell was commanding the troops, including one regiment of tanks, in the area of Sidi Rezegh ridge and the aerodrome. His small force holding this important ground was repeatedly attacked by large numbers of tanks and infantry. Wherever the situation was most difficult and the fighting hardest he was to be seen with his forward troops, either on his feet or in his open car. In this car he carried out general reconnaissance for counter-attacks by his tanks, whose senior officers had all become casualties early in the day. Standing in his car with a blue flag, this officer personally formed up tanks under close and intense fire from all natures of enemy weapons.

"On the following day the enemy attacks were intensified and again Brigadier Campbell was always in the forefront of the heaviest fighting, encouraging his troops, staging counter-attacks with his remaining tanks and personally controlling the fire of his guns. On two occasions he himself manned a gun to replace casualties. During the final enemy attack on November 22nd he was wounded, but continued most actively in the foremost positions, controlling the fire of the batteries, which inflicted heavy losses on enemy tanks at point-blank range, and finally acted as loader to one of the guns himself.

"Throughout these two days his magnificent example and his utter disregard of personal danger were an inspiration to his men and to all who saw him. His brilliant leadership was the direct cause of very heavy casualties inflicted on the enemy. In spite of his wound he refused to be evacuated and remained with his command, where his outstanding bravery and consistent determination had a marked effect in maintaining the splendid fighting spirit of those under him."

GEORGE GUNN (1912–1941)

2nd Lieutenant George Ward Gunn MC — Royal Horse Artillery.

"On November 21st 1941, at Sidi Rezegh, 2nd Lt Gunn was in command of a troop of four anti-tank guns which was part of a battery of 12 guns attached to the Rifle Brigade Column. At ten o'clock a covering force of enemy tanks was engaged and driven off, bu an hour later the main attack by about 60 enemy tanks developed. 2nd Lt Gunn drove from gun to gun during this period in an unarmoured vehicle encouraging his men and reorganising his dispositions as first one gun and then another were knocked out. Finally, only two guns remained in action and were subjected to very heavy fire. Immediately afterwards one of these guns was destroyed and the portee of the other was set on fire and all the crew killed or wounded except the sergeant, though the gun remained undamaged. The battery commander then arrived and began to fight the flames. When he saw this, 2nd Lt Gunn ran to his aid through intense fire and immediately got the one remaining anti-tank gun into action on the burning portee, himself sighting it whilst the sergeant acted as loader. He continued to fight the gun, firing between 40 and 50 rounds regardless alike of the enemy fire which was by then concentrated on this one vehicle and on the flames which might at any moment have reached the ammunition with which the portee was loaded. In spite of this, 2nd Lt Gunn's shooting was so accurate at a range of about 800 yards that at least two enemy tanks were hit and set on fire and others were damaged before he fell dead, having been shot through the forehead."

JOHN BEELEY (1918–1941)

Citation of Rifleman John Beeley, 1st Battalion The King's Royal Rifle Corps

"On the 21st November 1941, during the attack at Sidi Rezegh, against a strong enemy position, the company to which Rifleman Beeley belonged was pinned down by heavy fire at point-blank range from the front and flank on the flat, open ground of the aerodrome. All the officers but one of the company and many other ranks had either been killed or wounded. On his own initiative, and when there was no sort of cover, Rifleman Beeley got to his feet carrying a Bren gun and ran forward towards a strong enemy post. He ran thirty yards and discharged a complete magazine at the post from a range of twenty yards, killing or wounding the entire crew of the anti-tank gun. The post was silenced and Rifleman Beeley's platoon was able to advance, but Rifleman Beeley fell dead across his gun, hit in at least four places.

"Rifleman Beeley went to certain death in a gallant and successful attempt to carry the day. His courage and self-sacrifice were a glorious example to his comrades and inspired them to further efforts to reach their objective, which they eventually captured, together with 700 prisoners."

POSTWAR

Above: Postwar, Soltau in North Germany, near a large British-run training area on the Lüneberge Heide, south of Hamburg, became the "Desert Rats" HQ location for many years once 7th Armd Bde assumed the 7th Armd Div Rat as its shoulder flash in place of the Green Rat. Now, with the slimming down of British forces in Germany, the Bde HQ has been moved to Hohne, where much of the British armour is concentrated.

Above right: A "Desert Rat" tank commander in his turret during Operation Desert Sabre, in which 7th Armd Bde was in the British 1st Armoured Division as part of the United Nations forces which went to the rescue of Kuwait. The main ground assault began at 0400hrs on 24 February 1991, the British and American armour swiftly making short work of Saddam Hussein's much vaunted Republican Guard.

1945-8

During the initial postwar years 7th Armoured Division remained an integral part of the British Army of the Rhine (BAOR), with its units spread around North Rhine Westphalia and its divisional headquarters in the village of Bad Rothenfelde. Maj-Gen "Pip" Roberts CB, DSO, MC had been commanding since January 1946 and had guided the division through the initial, difficult period of "Army of Occupation" duties. Although Gen "Pip" had commanded 11th Armoured Division in the latter stages of the war, he was no stranger to 7th Armoured, having been a "Desert Rat" for most of the North African campaign, his last appointment with the division being as commander of 22nd Armoured Brigade at the time of the capture of Tripoli. The *Army Quarterly* of the day described him as being: "the living embodiment of all that has been best in the Division", therefore it was sad that he should have been commanding when, for the first time, the division was disbanded in March 1948.

In his farewell message to his "Desert Rats" Gen Roberts had expressed the hope that the division would be reformed and, fortunately, his words proved to be prophetic. About the time of the end of the Berlin airlift and the beginning of the Cold War (mid-1949), the division was reformed and went on to serve with distinction in BAOR until 16 April 1958, when it was yet again disbanded. However, on this occasion it was a change of title only, being redesignated first as the "5th Division" and then under a year later as the "1st Division" — the inner workings of the MOD never fail to amaze! A leader in *The Times* newspaper, published on the day following its disbandment, extolled the virtues of the remarkable "Desert Rats", stating that they had: "… won more renown than any other division has ever gained in the history of the British Army", then going on to explain why this was the case as they had been "first in and last out", being on active operations in the Western Desert at the start of the war. Winston Churchill certainly had a soft spot for his "Dear Desert Rats" as he called them, however, this did not save them and, as *The Times* ended its leader: "Public Relations are important, in war as in anything else. The nickname of the 'Desert Rats' caught on. It is a lesson which the unimaginative generals who had decreed the end of this famous fighting force should take to heart."

COLD-WAR DAYS

But of course that was not the end, because you cannot keep a good "Rat" down for long! The "Desert Rats" went on living in the shape of 7th Armoured Brigade (now wearing the Red Rat), still in BAOR, with its headquarters at Soltau. All "Rat" property, silver, pictures and relics were kept there and annually the Brigade celebrated the Battle of Sidi Rezegh on 22 November. Also, a 7th Armoured Division Officers Dinner Club was formed and met regularly each year in London. It seemed as though the "Rat" was indestructible although the "Powers that Be" certainly tried their best! In 1975 the Defence White Paper announced that brigades would be no more, but fortunately this was never put into practice thanks to the Cold War.

For the next quarter of a century war was prevented by the certain knowledge of the terrible consequences that would follow any attack by either side, in the shape of the subsequent nuclear exchange. The "Shield and Sword" of NATO contained tanks as an essential component of both, as did its Warsaw Pact potential enemies. With the demise of the Iron Curtain it had been hoped that disarmament talks would produce a great turning of "swords into ploughshares" once both sides had agreed to drastic arms limitations. However, whilst the head-to-head West versus East Europe problems have lessened, the modern world has proven to be just as dangerous a place, especially in the two major problem areas of the Middle East and the Balkans. Both have involved the United Nations in either peace-keeping operations or all-out war. The invasion of Kuwait in early August 1990, led first to Desert Shield, followed by Desert Storm, with a massive build-up of Coalition forces in the Gulf in order to take on Saddam Hussein's militant Iraq, in what he promised would be the "Mother of All Battles". A major part of the British contingent was 1 (British) Armoured Division, which comprised both 4th Armoured (The Black Rat) and 7th Armoured (The Red Rat) as its main components. Thus it was that the little jerboas were back in their desert setting. Both brigade groups had whirlwind success in the battle, which turned out to be something of a "damp squib", the Iraqi forces — estimated at the time to be the fourth largest army in the world — caving in, once the ground attack began in earnest. It was estimated that some 4,000 enemy tanks were destroyed in the 100-hour battle that brought the 43-day campaign to a close, the sheer professionalism of the two British brigades showing that they had still all the skills that had made their forefathers so successful.

OPERATION TELIC

The second Gulf War lasted from 19 March to 20 April 2003, the end result being the collapse of the Saddam Hussein regime. This time the Coalition forces went "all the way", effectively destroying Saddam's power base. Leading the assault on the second most important city in Iraq — Basra — was the 7th Armoured Brigade, its Challenger 2 tanks once again emblazoned with the little red desert rat that has come to symbolise all that is best in armoured warfare

Above: The "Desert Rat" in Bosnia. As the millennium closed, units of 7th Armd Bde went off to Bosnia on Operation Agricola. Here the crew of a 2 RTR Scimitar keeps a sharp lookout for interlopers from an OP on high ground some 800m from the Macedonian-Kosovo border. *Tank*

The Scarlet Rat is there again! This time the brigade sign is emblazoned on the front of the commanding officer of 2 RTR's Challenger 2, as it is photographed near Podujevo in Bosnia, February 2001. *Tank*

ASSESSMENT

WORLD WAR II

Apart from the one hiccup at Villers Bocage and its aftermath, the 7th Armoured Division had a wartime record second to none. Other divisions may well have felt that this was unfair, that they had won equally glorious victories and fought under even worse conditions, but the 7th Armoured was undoubtedly the only armoured division to acquire a reputation in the Army equivalent to that of "The Few" in the RAF. Indeed, the entire Eighth Army was happy to bask in its reflected glory and to call themselves "Desert Rats", despite the fact that only the units that were bona fide members of the division actually wore the little red jerboa. "The Desert Rats preserved a shining spirit," wrote the leader writer in *The Times* newspaper, on the day after the division was initially disbanded in March 1948. He continued: "rightly or wrongly, the concept of chivalry was retained among them in the circumstances of modern war. They were a light-hearted and happy division. Sir Winston Churchill in his memoirs recounts how, listening in London to a relay of one of the early desert battles, he heard with delight a squadron leader report: 'I am now at the second "B" in Buq Buq.' They exemplified the attitude of the British to war at its most dangerous, which found a response among the British people." They were clearly also helped by the inspired choice of emblem, the symbolism was there from the very start and remains as fresh today as it was in the early desert days. 7th Armoured Division was further immortalised by Jon's unforgettable cartoons — there was clearly only one division that the "Two Types" could have served in, and thus its reputation was enhanced by humour. And rightly so.

In North Africa, after helping to dispose of the inept Italians, the "Desert Rats" had found themselves up against other highly professional soldiers in the shape of the *Deutsches Afrika Korps*. In some ways they were very similar — was there, for

Below: Travels of the "Desert Rat" during WW2 are shown on this map

PETROL CONSUMPTION

During periods of heavy fighting the RASC carried 300 tons of ammunition and 150 tons of petrol each day. During periods of fast movement, ammunition was reduced to 150 tons and petrol raised to 360 tons per day. Even when the division was completely static it used 30,000 gallons of petrol per day. The Petrol Company lifted 69,245 tons of petrol between D-Day and 5 May 1945, which was an average of 466 lifts per lorry. B Platoon of the Petrol Company, which was equipped with four and a half ton Mack lorries, covered 462,000 miles, which was an average of 14,000 miles per vehicle.

AMMUNITION EXPENDITURE

General Verney, in *The Desert Rats*, identified these figures for ammunition expenditure 6 June 1944–5 May 1945.

RHA 25pdr HE

June–September: 295,700 rounds (average 51 per gun per day)
October–December: 104,400 (average 28 per gun per day)
January–May: 149,168 (average 26 per gun per day)
Total: 549,268

Tanks 17pdr HE

June–September: 13,000 rounds (average 3,250 per month)
October–December: 19,807 (average 6,602 per month)
January–May: 18,918 (average 4,729 per month)
Total: 51,725

4.2in Mortar HE

June–September: 5,248 rounds (average 1,312 per month)
October–December: 5,024 (average 1,674 per month)
January–May: 10,056 (average 2,514 per month)
Total: 20,328

.303in Rifle

June–September: 306,300 rounds (average 76,575 per month)
October–December: 376,000 (average 125,333 per month)
January–May: 464,300 (average 116,075 per month)
Total: 1,146,600

example, another senior German general who, like Rommel, wore a check scarf with his uniform, not unlike the gaudy, but very sensible, neckerchiefs, worn by many officers of the "Desert Rats"? The mutual respect which each side had for the other was undoubtedly matched by the chivalry that was so often displayed. The British respected Rommel, the "Desert Fox", and his men, and this was reflected by the DAK.

Villers Bocage

I have deliberately not laboured the disastrous action at Villers Bocage, principally because a full explanation deserves far more space than I can give in this short book. However, it is only fair to state the background facts as they apply. First and foremost, one must remember the situation that pertained in the UK when 7th Armoured Division arrived home from Italy in late 1943. Many of the soldiers had not been home since before the war and had just fought an extremely hard campaign in North Africa and again in Italy, while the rest of the "D-Day Army" had been training in the relative safety of the United Kingdom. Some of them undoubtedly felt that it was time for others to take the risks and said so, which did not go down well, raising a tricky morale problem for Gen Erskine. Add to this the fact that a fair number of the division's most experienced officers and men were taken away to provide battle-experience within other units and formations. Additionally, and probably most worrying of all, the division had been forced to exchange its tried and trusted Sherman Medium tanks for much smaller, less-well armoured cruisers, ie the Cromwell, of which most soldiers were deeply suspicious — it was less mechanically reliable and did not even mount a decent larger-calibre gun, so they would still be outgunned by the enemy. The Sherman Firefly, with its highly effective 17-pounder, was issued only on the scale of one per troop, so it was 3 to 1 against it being in the right place at the right time unless it always led. Thus, whilst Michael Wittmann's almost complete destruction of 7th Armoured Division's entire advance guard at Villers Bocage, was a superlative piece of individual tank commanding, the Cromwells were "sitting ducks" as compared with the massive 56-ton Tiger and its highly lethal 88mm gun that could easily penetrate the front armour of a Cromwell at long range, yet was impervious to its return fire, even at very short range.

Fighting in the bocage. 7th Armoured also found itself in a very different environment to the desert, or for that matter to Italy, and took time to adapt, as Gen Sir Brian Horrocks commented in his autobiography: "Another disturbing feature was the comparative lack of success of the veteran 7th Armoured and 51st Highland Divisions. Both came again later on and finished the war in magnificent shape, but during the Normandy fighting they were not at their best. ... after being lionised in the UK, (they) came out to Normandy and found themselves faced with an entirely different type of battle, fought under different conditions of terrain. And they began to see the difficulties all too clearly. A racing enthusiast once described this condition to me as 'like an old plater who won't go in the mud'. All the more credit to them that they eventually staged a come-back and regained their Middle East form." However, the division's problems did not entirely end with Villers Bocage and dragged on for some weeks. The outcome was that "Monty" had to remove the XXX Corps commander (Bucknall) and two divisional commanders — Erskine of 7th Armoured and Bullen-Smith of 51 Infantry, as he put it in a letter to a friend: "I have had to get rid of a few people you know. Bucknall could not manage a Corps once the battle became mobile and I have Jorrocks (General Horrocks) in his place in XXX Corps. Bullen-Smith could do nothing with 51 Div so had to go; Thomas Rennie is there now and the Division is quite different under him. 7 Armd Div went right down and failed badly; so I removed Bobbie (Erskine) who had become very sticky and put in Verney of the Gds Tank brigade. I also had to remove Loony Hinde; I have put Mackeson to 23 Armd Bde." In an earlier letter he had written to US Gen Simpson: "The old deser divisions are apt to look over their shoulders and wonder if all is OK behind or if the flanks are secure and so on. 7 Armoured Div is like that. They want a new General who will drive them headlong into and through gaps torn in enemy defence — not worrying about flanks or anything … We want Generals now who will put their heads down and go like hell."

That then is the only minor blemish on the "Desert Rats'" escutcheon and, once "sorted" by Montgomery's drastic action, they recovered superbly.

POSTWAR

Postwar, the little "red rat" has done it again, especially in the second Gulf War, the latest "war by television", during which all ranks of the 7th Armoured Brigade have exuded sheer professionalism and quiet confidence. Whenever they have been asked to talk "On the Box", their ancestors would be proud of them! Challenger 2 is, of course, a far more sophisticated animal than a Sherman or Comet of World War II, however, it has warmed the heart of this old "tankie" to see that they still at times look more like "tinkers carts" than sleek, lethal weapons of war because of all the added "goodies" that the crews have acquired to make desert life just that little bit more comfortable as they go "Up the Blue". Undoubtedly, the general public has once again taken the "Desert Rats" to its heart, giving their exploits much well-deserved coverage.

Below: "Dear Desert Rats!" Prime Minister Winston Churchill addresses some of the division at the opening of its club in Berlin. *IWM — BU9111*

CONCLUSION

Perhaps the best way in which to close this book is with the words of Winston Churchill when he spoke to men of the division in Berlin after the Victory Parade on 21 July 1945, at the opening of the "Winston Club": "It is not without emotion that I can express to you what I feel about the 'Desert Rats'. Dear 'Desert Rats'! May your glory ever shine! May your laurels never fade! May the memory of this glorious pilgrimage of war which you have made from Alamein, via the Baltic to Berlin, never die! It is a march unsurpassed through all the story of war so far as my reading of history leads me to believe. May the fathers long tell the children about this tale. May you all feel that in following your great ancestors you have accomplished something which has done good to the whole world; which has raised the honour of your own country and which every man has a right to be proud of."

REFERENCE

WEBSITES

http://houterman.htmlplanet.com/7Armd Div.html
Website giving unit histories, in this case 7th Armoured.

www.army.mod.uk/7bde/
Information on the modern "Desert Rats" — 7th Armoured Brigade.

www.fmdinning.freeserve.co.uk
Photos and information on the Thetford Forest Memorial.

www.btinternet.com/~ian.a.paterson/main.htm
Website devoted to the history of the "Desert Rats".

www.regiments.org/milhist/uk/lists/badivxref.htm
Website that gives details of the "Land Forces of Britain, the Empire and Commonwealth" including divisional histories.

BIBLIOGRAPHY

Carver, Lt-Col R. M. P.: *A Short History of the Seventh Armoured Division, October 1938–May 1943*, Printing & Stationery Services MEF, 1943.
Lt-Col (Later Field Marshal, Lord) Mike Carver, late Royal Tank Regiment, served with HQ 7th Armd Div early in the war and later commanded 1 RTR in 22 Armd Bde, so his knowledge of the division was second to none. He was also a brilliant historian and has written many books. His memoirs, *Out of Step* (Hutchinson, 1989), are well worth reading, especially as much of the book is relevant to the "Desert Rats".

Cordingley, Maj-Gen Patrick: *In the Eye of the Storm — Commanding the Desert Rats in the Gulf War*, Hodder & Stoughton, 1996.
A good, honest, first-hand account of his brigade's part in the first Gulf War, when he was commanding 7th Armd Bde.

Delaforce, Patrick: *Churchill's Desert Rats, from Normandy to Berlin with the 7th Armoured Division*, Allan Sutton Publishing, 1994.
Churchill's Desert Rats 2: 7th Armoured Division in North Africa, Burma, Sicily and Italy,

Alan Sutton Publishing, 2002.
Delaforce, a Horse Gunner, served in 11 Armd Div during the war, then joined 7th Armoured (3 RHA) postwar. He has since written many books, mostly in the same style, that is to say, full of fascinating reminiscences and glimpses of battle, all providing very useful background reading.

Ellis, Chris: *Spearhead 1 21st Panzer Division — Rommel's Afrika Korps Spearhead*, Ian Allan Publishing, 2001.
Good all-round coverage of the principal opponent to the Desert Rats, the German 21st Panzer Division which fought through the desert before being destroyed around Tunis in 1943. It would be reconstituted to fight in Normandy after D-Day and was annihilated at Falaise.

Forty, George: *Desert Rats at War — North Africa*, Ian Allan Publishing, 1975.
Desert Rats at War — Europe, Ian Allan Publishing , 1977.
Tank Commanders, Knights of the Modern Age, Firebird, 1993.
Tanks across the Desert — the war diary of Sgt Jake Wardrop, Sutton Publishing, 2003.
Again, these are mainly "I was there"-type reporting, with lots of relevant, private photographs and first-hand accounts. *Tank Commanders, Knights of the Modern Age*, however, covers the entire history of armoured warfare from the invention of the first tank to the first Gulf War in 1990-1.

Lindsay, Capt Martin and Johnston, Capt M. E.: *History of 7th Armoured Division, June 1943–July 1945.* Originally published and printed in BAOR in 1945. Reprinted in 2001 by DP&G on behalf of the Tank Museum, which is now the copyright holder for this book.
This is really the continuation of Mike Carver's book and is a straightforward, factual account of the history of the "Desert Rats" from Italy up to the end of the war. The photographs are only photocopies, but the originals are available via the IWM Dept of Photos.

Neillands, Robin: *The Desert Rats: 7th Armoured Division, 1940-45*, Weidenfeld & Nicolson, 1991.
A good, general account of the wartime history of the 7th Armoured Division by a well-known military author.

Pearce, Nigel: *The Shield and the Sabre: the Desert Rats in the Gulf 1990-91*, HMSO, 1992.
Background reading, specifically about the Gulf War.

Sandars, John and Chappell, Mike: *British 7th Armoured Division 1940-45*, Osprey Vanguard series No 1, 1977.
Osprey — Vanguard1, published in 1977. This early volume in a well-loved series of flexiback books, gives a brief, but valuable, potted history of the division and all its works, with the usual emphasis on badges and insignia.

Verney, Maj Gen G L: *The Desert Rats*, Hutchinson, 1954. Reprinted in hardback, with new Introduction by General Sir John Hackett, in 1996 by Greenhill Books. Reprinted in paperback by Greenhill Books in 2002.
Without doubt, the best and most comprehensive "straight" history of the division,

Above: The battered walls of Fort Capuzzo, one of the desert forts, situated to the west of Sollum and the south of Bardia. It was built by the Italians prewar and changed hands many times. Here scout carriers of 1 KRRC, 7th Armd Div Support Group, congregate outside one of its gateways.

Right: A9 cruisers of 1 RTR, moving through the outskirts of Cairo on their way "Up the Blue", 30 May 1940. Although the majority of the vehicle's tell-tale signs have been blotted out by the censor on this photograph, the Mobile Division's white circle on its scarlet background is still visible.

written by one of its GOCs. Verney was a "no-nonsense" Guardsman and his book provides a first-rate, detailed history of the "Desert Rats" in World War II.

Additional books which contain information or reminiscences about 7th Armd Div units are listed below. They can provide valuable detail if needed, but many are detailed Regimental Histories and contain a lot of irrelevant information. *Take These Men* by Cyril Joly, however, is without doubt one of the best books about tank crews in action in wartime and is highly recommended.

Bolitho, Hector: *The Galloping Third*, John Murray, 1963.

Clark, Dudley: *The Eleventh at War*, Michael Joseph, 1952.

Crawford, Robert: *I was an Eighth Army Soldier*, Victor Gollancz, 1944.

Davy, George: *The Seventh & Three Enemies*, Heffer, 1952.

Evans, Roger: *The Story of the Fifth Royal Inniskilling Dragoon Guards*, Gale & Polden, 1951.

Foster, R. C. G.: *History of the Queen's Royal Regiment Volume 8*, Gale & Polden, 1956.

Hart, B. Liddell: *The Tanks, Volume 2*, Cassell, 1959.

Hastings, R. H. W. S.: *The Rifle Brigade in the Second World War 1939-1945,* Gale & Polden, 1949.

Joly, Cyril: *Take these Men,* Constable, 1955.

Nicol, A. A.: *My Moving Tent: Diary of a Desert Rat,* Pentland, 1994.

Watt, Maj Robin: *A Soldier's Sketch-book: with the British Army in the Gulf,* National Army Museum, 1994.

Woolley, A. D.: *The History of the KDG,* Privately published, 1946.

MEMORIALS

The Memorial Stone
In addition to the still-operational 7th Armoured Brigade, there are some other tangible reminders of the "Desert Rats", one being a memorial stone detailing the countries through which the division fought on its triumphal path from El Alamein to Berlin (1939-45). It was erected at the end of the autobahn near Berlin when the division entered the city in the summer of 1945. However, it was moved to the grounds of the Royal Military Academy, Sandhurst, where it still stands.

The Thetford Forest Memorial
At the entrance to the Covert site near Swaffham, Norfolk, stands a tank memorial to the "Desert Rats". The site is close to their wartime camp in which they spent the period January-May 1944, preparing for the D-Day invasion of Normandy. The memorial comprises a Cromwell tank, from which footpaths connect to the campsites at High Ash Wood, Shakers Wood and Sugar Hill.

INDEX

Ashworth, J. B. 50
Auchinleck, Sir Claude 23, 24
Avalanche, Operation 36

Battleaxe, Operation 22–3
Baytown, Operation 37
Beda Fomm 19, 21, 72, 80
Beeley, John 24, 85
Beresford-Pierse, Sir Noel 18, 22
Blackcock, Operation 61
Brevity, Operation 22–3
British and Commonwealth units: **Armies** — First, 31; Eighth, 23, 27, 31, 36, 37, 51, 81, 89; **Brigades** — 1st Commando 60, 61; 4th Armoured 9, 11, 14, 18, 19, 22, 23, 24, 26, 51, 52, 66, 67, 87; 4th Light, 30; 8th Armoured, 60; 22nd Armoured 23, 24, 25, 30, 36, 37, 39, 40, 41, 42, 43, 47, 48, 50, 51, 57, 62, 64, 66, 68, 83, 86; 131st (Queens), 30, 31, 36, 41, 49, 52, 55, 57, 60, 64, 66; 155th Infantry, 60; **Corps** — I, 45; VIII, 48, 55; X, 37, 39; XII, 51, 55, 57, 60, 61; XIII, 18, 23, 24, 25, 39, 50, 51, 80; XXX, 24, 25, 43, 45, 48, 49, 50, 61, 90; **Divisions** —Australian 6th, 18; 9th, 20; Canadian 2nd, 49; 3rd, 49; 5th 39; British — Guards Armored, 49, 55; 2nd Armoured, 20; 6th Armoured, 57; 11th Armoured 49, 55, 80, 81, 83; 46th Infantry, 37, 39; 50th Infantry 43, 57; 51st Infantry 51, 90; 52nd Infantry, 60; 53rd Infantry, 62; 56th Infantry, 37, 39; 79th Armored, 80; Indian — 4th, 15, 18, 22, 26, 81; **Regiments and Battalions** — 1 KRRC, 7, 8, 20, 85; 1 RTR, 6, 8, 9, 12, 13, 15, 37, 39, 48, 49, 50, 51, 52, 55, 60, 68, 69; 1 RTC, 6; 2 Devons 52, 57, 60; 2 RB 9, 81; 2 RTR, 65, 68, 69, 72, 87, 88; 3 CLY 48; 3 Coldstream Guards 20; 3 H 20; 3 RHA, 6, 8, 9, 50, 60, 62, 64; 4 CLY 42, 45, 48, 49; 4 RHA, 8, 9, 16; 4 RTR, 22; 1/5 Queens 50, 52, 57, 60, 61, 62, 64; 5 Inniskilling Dragoon Guards, 47, 48, 49, 50, 51, 52, 61, 62, 64; 5 RHA, 36; 5 RTR, 26, 39, 43, 48, 49, 50, 52, 59, 61, 62, 68; 1/6 Queens 39, 50, 51; 6 RHA, 50; 6 RTR, 6, 8, 18, 20, 22, 77; 7 Queens Own Hussars, 6, 8, 65; 1/7 Queens 37, 50, 51, 57; 7

RTR, 18, 22, 64; 8 Kings Royal Irish Hussars, 6, 8, 18, 40, 49, 52, 55, 57, 61, 62, 64; 9 Durham Light Infantry, 57, 60, 61, 62; 10 Medical, 51; 11 H (Prince Albert's Own) 6, 8, 9, 12, 16, 19, 20, 30, 35, 36, 40, 50, 51, 55, 59, 61, 62, 64, 66, 68, 83, 86; 1 RB, 52, 55, 61;
Brooke, Sir Alan 62
Bucknall, Gerald 45, 48, 82, 90

Campbell, "Jock" 16, 24, 26, 81, 84
Caunter, "Blood" 9, 80
Chater, Robin 7
Churchill, Winston 8, 22, 26, 34, 62, 64, 80, 89
Cobra, Operation 49
Compass, Operation 15, 16–8
Creagh, Michael O'Moore 8, 9, 66, 80
Crocker, Sir John 45
Crusader, Operation 23
Cunningham, Sir Alan 23, 24

D-Day 45
Dempsey, Sir Miles 45

El Alamein 15, 27, 30–33, 81, 83, 91, 95
Erskine, Sir George 40, 48, 82, 90

Gatehouse, Alec 81
Gazala 2, 25, 26–30, 81
German units: **Armies** — Fifteenth, 54; **Divisions** — 5th leichte, 20, 22; 7th (Ghost) Panzer, 20; 15th Panzer, 20, 22; 21st Panzer, 30; Deutsches Afrika Korps, 4, 20, 25, 31, 33, 89, 90, 93
Gordon-Finlayson, Sir Robert 7, 8
Gott, "Strafer" 20, 23, 26, 72, 80, 81
Gunn, George 24, 84

Harding, Lord, of Petherton 31, 82
Hart, Sir Basil Liddell 80
Hedley, Jerry 32
Hitler, Adolf 20
Hobart, Pat 37
Hobart, Sir Percy 6, 7, 8, 16, 43, 80, 81
Horrocks, Sir Brian 31, 48, 90
Husky, Operation 36
Hussein, Saddam 87

Italian units: **Armies** —Tenth, 19; **Divisions** — Ariete, 20, 24; Brescia, 20

Kesselring, Albert 37

Lyne, Lewis 57, 61, 62, 82, 83
Lyon, Hugh 35

March, John 19
Market Garden, Operation 55–60
Messervy, Frank 26, 81
Mews, R. 48
Mirrles, W. H. B. 8
Montgomery, Bernard 27, 30, 32, 42, 47, 62, 83
Mussolini, Benito 6, 10

O'Connor, Sir Richard 8, 15, 16, 18, 19, 20, 48, 82
Operations: Avalanche, 36; Battleaxe, 22–3; Baytown, 37; Blackcock, 61; Brevity, 22–3; Cobra, 49; Compass, 15, 16–8; Crusader, 23; Husky, 36; Market Garden, 55–60; Perch, 43; Plunder, 61; Venezia, 26

Perch, Operation 43
Plunder, Operation 61

Renton, "Wingy" 81
Ritchie, Sir Neil 24, 26, 51
Roberts, "Pip" 81, 82, 83, 86
Rommel, Erwin 2, 20, 21, 23, 24, 25, 26, 27, 30, 31, 33, 43, 88, 93
Russell, H. E. 6, 8

Sidi Rezegh 15, 23, 24, 25, 27, 81, 84, 85, 86
Smail, A. J. 35
Suez Canal 6, 20, 27

US units: **Armies** — Fifth, 36, 37

Venezia, Operation 26
Verney, Gerald 9, 11, 48, 49, 50, 51, 54, 57, 67, 82, 83
Victoria Cross 16, 24, 81, 84–5
Victory, Paddy 47
Villers Bocage 43, 45, 47, 48, 50, 82, 83, 89, 90

Watkins, "Boomer" 8
Wavell, Sir Archibald 8, 15, 19, 20, 22, 25
Western Desert Force 8, 11, 16, 18
Wilson, "Jumbo" 8
Wittman, Michael 47